GOD'S
Will and Testament

T.S.S.

ISBN 978-1-64003-088-6 (Paperback)
ISBN 978-1-64003-089-3 (Digital)

Covenant Books, Inc.
11661 Hwy 707
Murrells Inlet, SC 29576
www.covenantbooks.com

The God of mystery

The mystery of the gospel of Jesus Christ is the greatest, most clouded, and most contended words that are in print. Every one of every denomination of the Christian religion has their own way of interpreting the same words. They all say that their version or translation of the scripture is the only correct one. How can this be? One version of the Bible says, "He that overcomes," and another says, "Everyone that overcomes." One is speaking of a single masculine subject, and the other is saying the subject is gender neutral and plural. Another version adds a whole bunch of extra words and sentences, and another version leaves out whole words and sentences. This confusion has to end.

The remedy is simpler than you could imagine now that we have computers and the Internet. All you have to do is go to a Bible website where you can parallel read a version of the Bible's New Testament with the original Greek. After you do that and see the insane deviations of the translations, you will conclude that the most accurate and true to the original text is the King James Version. It is the only version I use and the only version anyone should ever use.

A singular masculine noun in the Greek is translated into a singular masculine noun in English, and so on. This word-by-word accuracy to the original text is mandatory to unveil the hidden mystery of the scripture because it is written with the letter-by-letter accuracy of a legal document, which is God's old will and testament and new will and testament.

By the way, the word *testament* means "a will"—not "Will you do that?" but, rather, a "will and testament." Since a fool is known by his many words, the scripture is written as a wise man speaks: few words but with greater meaning and that not only intensifies the power of a sentence. It leaves no room to make a lie or falsify the meaning.

It is also important to note that unless you look at your faith as through the eyes of a child, you cannot enter the kingdom of God. Jesus used the word *cannot*, and that is a very simple and strong statement. Since we know that our faith comes from reading the word of God, we see that we must read scripture like a child does when learning the construction of sentences. We can also see the implied meaning, which is if we do look at the scripture as a child, then we will enter the kingdom.

Remember that the kingdom is neither here nor there, but it is within you. It is the knowledge of the truth of God. Jesus said in John 6:40 that "everyone which sees the son, and believes on him, may have everlasting life: and I will raise him up at the last day."

Now throw away what religion has taught you and look at this sentence as though you were in grammar school as a child: "Everyone that sees the Son," okay; "and believes on him," okay; *him* refers to the masculine noun previously mentioned which is the Son "may have everlasting life," okay; so far so good, "and I will raise him up at the last day," okay; and *him* is still referring to the Son. So, what this verse is saying is that Jesus will raise the Son up at the last day.

Wait a minute! All the church leaders have been telling us that this means Jesus will raise all of us up at the resurrection at the end of the world, but that is not what the scripture is saying! Hold on, he says it again in John 6:44: "No man [no one] can come to me, except the Father which has sent me draw him [*draw* means "choose," like *draw a card* means "take one card"], and I will raise him up at the last day."

We have two things going on with "raise him up." *Raise* has dual meanings like "raise a child up" and "raise him up from the dead." Now, watch this, it gets better and clearer in John 6:50 when he says, "This is the bread which cometh down from heaven, that a man (one

4

man) may eat thereof, *and not die.*' He said that "he is the bread that one man may eat and not die?" Religious teachers have been telling us that this means that everybody who believes in him will be resurrected and live forever, but he doesn't mention anything like that here. He states it very clearly and simply and with very few words in this verse: if one man digests his words, he will not die.

Jesus is quite the character because he really wanted to drive this home so they all would understand, but they didn't. They thought he was speaking of literally eating his flesh instead of figuratively digesting and understanding his sayings. He said it again in John 6:54, but the grand finale is in John 6:58, saying, "Not like your fathers ate manna and are dead, but the same singular *he* **that eats this bread** *shall live forever*" [italics mine]. Now, **take a few minutes and read the book of John starting at about verse John 6:30 and up to verse John 6:60. If you see and understand the aforementioned explanation of the words that construct the sentences, which now have a totally new meaning, then you are not far from understanding the kingdom!**

It is pretty shocking to learn that you have been misled your whole life by people in positions of authority, especially when it comes to learning about God. I remember fifteen years ago when I was first shown these things and shocked out of my skin, and I was so thirsty for more! You read the verse, and your mind has that pre-programmed false understanding that you were raised with, and then your eyes are opened to the truth within the meanings of the words that you learned as a child. This is where you have to use your own reasoning whether to believe man or God, not to mention using a great big, thick dictionary!

Scripture says that I would rather every man be a liar and the word of God be truth. I just never imagined that it would get this out of control where even that has come to pass! My favorite line to use on false teachers is this: "If everyone that calls upon the name of the lord shall be saved then what is his new name?" (Rom. 10:13–14). This is a legitimate and justifiable question to ask.

Jesus said to the one who overcomes that he would write his new name on him, so what is it? (Rev. 3:12). This question drives the wicked insane because it implies the knowledge of the heir to the throne in God's will and testament: the book of Revelation. You see, Jesus said himself that the things concerning him have an end (Luke 22:37). This is hidden in plain sight in Revelation 3:21 and is written using the words of a legal will and testament: "To him that overcometh *will I grant* to sit with me in my throne" [italics mine].

I can't explain this any simpler! To the one whom this is granted is the executor of God's will and testament. This is the lamb who was slain in Revelation 5, who was worthy to take the book from him that sits on the throne from Jesus's right hand, which *is* God's will and testament, and execute it forever. What has kept it from being executed is the names of the heirs: you must have the heirs to the will present in order to read and execute it.

Fortunately, this copy of God's will and testament has the names of those who have the mark of the beast who are destroyed and those who have gotten the victory over the beast and his image and his mark and number and the name of the great city that is destroyed in one hour and the name of the bride of the lamb and the name of the heir to the throne of God, not to mention all the godly who are plainly named. Everybody is an heir to something, whether they are good or evil.

Can you imagine how the world would be if everyone understood that one of us would become this heir? It's not like Jesus didn't tell us by saying to love one another as you do yourself, don't lie, don't kill, and so on. The Jews have always believed that there is one person in each generation who has the potential to become the messiah, and that is pretty much what the scripture says: "Many are called but few are chosen" (Matt. 22:14, KJV). It's just that they use the same devises today that they used two thousand years ago with Jesus.

The Jews agreed already beforehand that if any man did confess that he was Christ, he should be put out of the synagogue (John 9:27). Does this make sense if you are looking for Christ to come? Wouldn't you want to question the person who says that, test the spirit so to speak, instead of throw him out of the church? Read on what the Bible says:

The chief priests and the Pharisees put together a counsel and said, "What do we do? If we leave him alone, everyone will believe in him, and the Romans will come and take away both our place and the nation." And then one of them named Caiaphas who was the high priest that year said, "You know nothing at all, nor consider that it is expedient for us that one man should die for the people, and that the whole nation perish not." He was saying that Jesus should die for the Jewish nation to continue as it was. Then from that day forth they took counsel together to put him to death. (John 11:47–53)

Then they said that it was expedient that one man should die for the people (John 18:14). They wanted to continue having rule over their nation and having the best seats in the synagogues and the high status and fancy clothes and position of authority among the people. Not too much different today. You cannot escape the cold, hard facts of the Bible, even if it seems difficult to digest.

Just take a look at Acts 13:6: "They found a certain sorcerer, a false prophet, a Jew, whose name was Barjesus," and then Acts 13:8: "But Elymas the sorcerer (for so is his name by interpretation) withstood them, seeking to turn away the deputy from the faith." Then Saul (Paul) had enough and said, "O full of all subtlety and all mischief, you child of the devil, you enemy of all righteousness, will you not cease to pervert the right ways of the Lord?" (Acts 13:10).

Sorcery is very real because the Bible says it is, and it is the way that the wicked still control the world. It began in the book of Genesis and is in the very last page of Revelation (22:15). I am by no means anti-Semitic; I am just revealing what the Bible says about some of the Jewish leaders thousands of years ago. The vast majority of them do not believe that Jesus Christ is the messiah for this very same reason: they would lose their place and status. It should also be noted that Jesus said that if you do not believe in him, you do not believe in him that sent him—God. If you do believe in him, you have both the Father and the Son.

The son of man is in heaven

No man has ascended up to heaven but he who came down from heaven, even the Son of man, which is in heaven. This is what Jesus said in John 3:13. This statement says that the Son of man whom he was beginning to reveal was still in heaven at the time Jesus was speaking on earth. To be totally accurate, any man or male child begotten or brought into existence of a man and woman is a son of man. So, you have to ask yourself, *Did a man and woman bring Jesus into existence?* Clearly the answer is no because God was the seed that fertilized the egg in his mother Mary, not Joseph.

To demonstrate this perfectly and eloquently, just turn to the first time the phrase is used in Numbers 23:19: "God is not a man, that he should lie; neither the son of man, that he should repent." Now, by studying this verse, we know that God is not a man or the son of man. Do not be confused at this—just always remember that we are looking into the mystery of God and the mystery of the gospel of Jesus Christ! It is a mystery to try to figure out what is hidden in the words. Jesus spoke a lot of parables for people to try to figure out, and most of the time the true meaning was hidden from the wise, but the common people heard him gladly. Even the eunuch who was asked if he understood the scripture he was reading in Acts 8:31 said, "How can I [understand], except some man should guide me?"

The answer to this little mystery is that Jesus was the only begotten Son of God, and he sometimes referred to himself sarcastically as the *son of man* to hide the mystery from the wise and prudent. This should be no surprise after reading how Jesus tied their brains in a knot when he asked, "How say they that Christ is David's son? And David himself saith in the book of Psalms, The LORD said unto my Lord, Sit thou on my right hand, till I make thine enemies thy footstool. David therefore calleth him Lord, how is he then his son?" (Luke 20:41–44).

This is just more of Jesus mocking them because they could not answer the question, and if they did answer, they would have to say that that cannot be so—Christ can't be David's son. The reality is that Jesus's whole ministry was to believe in him as the only begotten Son of God and in the last day he would raise a son of whom that God had chosen to inherit all things.

Now we come to the biggest hidden mystery in the most famous verse of the Bible, just three verses later: John 3:16. I would say that this verse is the most recognized verse around the world. It is amazing to me how everyone can explain a meaning of this verse and yet forget the meaning of the words that construct it. I showed you earlier how one word in John 6:40 changed the whole meaning of the sentence and that was the word *him* and how it refers to the Son who was previously mentioned, and not the word *everybody*.

The word *him* is singular, meaning "one male"; the word *he* is singular, also meaning "one male"; and the words *whoever, whosoever* are also singular but gender neutral. When you want to put a lot of emphasis on the word *whoever*, you say "whosoever." If I say, "Whoever wins the race gets the prize," do I mean everyone that runs the race gets the prize? No, only *the one who* wins the race gets the prize. If I look at a hundred racers and say, "Whoever comes in second place is the first loser," does it mean everyone? Does it mean the first ten who finish the race? No, it means *the one who* comes in second place. *Whoever* is always singular, meaning "one." It takes a bunch of extra words to make it plural and mean more than one.

For example, "Whoever comes here is my friend" means "one person." "Whoever does come here will be my friends" makes it plural, meaning "of many." So using these examples, we can accurately substitute the word *whosoever* with the meaning which is "the one who." We can also substitute the words *he, his,* and *him* for *God,* since it refers to God who is identified as the subject of the sentence previously mentioned. Now you can read this sentence and be enlightened with the biblical and grammatically accurate truth:

> For God so loved the world, that God gave
> his only begotten Son, that the one who belie-
> veth in God should not perish, but have everlast-
> ing life. (John 3:16)

This is another verse where Jesus, the spirit of prophecy, was telling us of the Son whom he would raise in the last day. *Everlasting* means "lasting forever and never coming to an end." Since this is prophesying of a future event, it is saying that at the end of the world, the people who are alive at the time when the Son is revealed, those people will not die and return again at the resurrection of the dead in Christ; and they will continue living forever if they see the Son he raises and believe in him. This cannot mean that Jesus is speaking about himself as the Son because then those people who were looking at him as he was saying this would not die, but they did die.

This is exactly what Jesus promised later in John 8:51 by saying that "if a man keep my saying, he shall never see death." Let me be clear—this is not a private interpretation of mine in any way, shape, or form. All I have done here is re-explain the things that you learned in grammar school when you were a child. We all used to, and for the most part still do, know the difference between singular and plural; masculine, feminine, and gender neutral; and so on. It is only through the sorcery and persuasion of the wicked that causes doubt and forgetting the basic rules of words when you read the scripture. It's the exact same tactic that the devil used in the garden when he spoke the first lie in contradiction to God. God said not to eat of the certain tree and "don't even touch it or you will die." And then along comes Satan and says, "No, you won't die," and then he charms Eve with a seducing spirit saying that she shall be as a god knowing good and evil, a promise of something better for breaking the rules.

From this point on, sorcery and lies have manifested as sin. This is why Jesus brought us the new will and testament of God to earth. "For this is my blood of the *new testament*, which is shed for many for the remission of sins" (Matt. 26:28; italics mine). He died for the remission of sins and said he would raise a son of man up in the last day, one who shall never see death, one who keeps his sayings, one who overcomes death as he did, the innocent lamb who was slain to redeem us to our God, and inherits all things (Rev. 21:7).

Jesus said "Behold, I come quickly" and "Behold, I come as a thief." Let's examine these closely, remembering that the answer lies within the pages of the scripture and not a private interpretation. Everybody seems to think they know what the scripture is saying by coming up with an elaborate fable to lead you astray. Always use 2 Peter 1:20 as a benchmark: "Knowing this first, that no prophecy of the scripture is of any private interpretation [a person's origin or understanding]."

You must be able to understand it by either checking it with other scripture or the interpretation will soon follow what needs to be interpreted or it is not prophecy. Remember that a child must be able to understand it as it is written. If a word used does not make sense in a sentence with a literal definition or a figurative definition, then it is not prophecy.

Behold, I come quickly. The first thing that comes to my mind is how Satan will try to accuse Jesus of not coming quickly enough. If he floated in the sky as in a fantastic fable of rapture, well, that's not very quickly; it could be quicker. Not to mention that is not how a thief would come, and rapture means intense love, ecstasy.

The words of Jesus written in red in Revelation 22:7 speak volumes: "Behold, I come quickly: blessed is *he* that keepeth the sayings of the prophecy of this book" [italics mine]. Remember earlier I showed you when he said "If a man keeps my sayings, he shall never see death"? Well, here in the book of Revelation, the book of God's will and testament, he is speaking of the same, one man. So when we turn toward this scripture, we see that he already came as fast as anyone could possibly come the first time he came; he was already here! He was walking around undercover, and that is exactly how he will return in the Son of man.

You see, the word *reveal* means to "uncover something previously hidden or kept a secret." First, something has to be hidden or covered in order for it to be revealed. So when Jesus said "Even thus shall it be in the day when the Son of man is revealed," it implies that he is already on earth undercover in the time that he is revealed (Luke

17:30). Earlier in Luke 17:25, he said that first the son must suffer many things and be rejected of this generation, and the keyword here is *generation*, which means everyone alive at the time. Did everyone alive reject Jesus at the time in his generation? No, he had disciples and plenty of people who believed in him as well as followers, so he was not speaking of himself.

Here is a verse to really open your eyes. Picture Jesus standing in front of a crowd of people and with his disciples when he says this: "All things are delivered to me of my Father: and *no man knoweth who the Son is*, but the Father; and who the Father is, but the Son, and he to whom the Son will reveal him" (Luke 10:22; italics mine). Now, using logic and reason, how can he be talking about himself being this Son in front of a crowd of people and say that no one knows the Son?

As if this isn't enough to amaze you into seeing the light, here is even a better example of him being under cover in the world in John 9:35–37:

> Jesus heard that they had cast him out [the blind guy he healed]; and when he had found him, he said unto him, Do you believe on the Son of God? He answered and said, who is he, Lord, that I might believe on him? And Jesus said unto him, *You have both seen him, and it is he that talketh with thee* [italics mine].

Now, take a moment and ponder that. Jesus was standing in front of a man and reveals that he is the Son of God! And as if that isn't enough to show you how cool Jesus was, take a look at John 4:25–26:

The woman saith unto him [Jesus], I know that Messiah cometh, which is called Christ: when he is come, he will tell us all things. Jesus saith unto her, *I that speak unto thee am he* [italics mine].

See? He revealed himself again! He uncovered what was covered. Jesus was not the only Son of God; he was the only *begotten* Son of God. His genealogy on his mother's side went all the way back to Adam, the son of God (Luke 3:38). And in Genesis 6:2 it says, "That the sons of God saw the daughters of men that they were fair; and they took them wives of all which they chose." This word *sons* is plural, so we can't put a number on the sons of God. But there is only *one* begotten Son of God—Jesus.

Begotten in this sense means "he was brought into existence by God," a human woman but not a human father. He was also the first begotten of the dead, and in this sense, *begotten* means "to obtain"— for example, "success begets more success"; he was the first to obtain immortality through death and show us that the word of God is true.

All these verses show us how fast he came quickly; so quick that it can't be done any quicker, lest he be accused of not coming quick enough, and that's the way he returns. Now let's see how he will come as a thief like he came the first time: "Behold, I come as a thief" (Rev. 16:15) Does this mean that he is going to literally return to earth disguised as a thief? Well, the word *as* does mean "to the same amount or degree of something," so, yes. The lamb that was slain in Revelation and Jesus, the Lamb of God, were not literally lambs. "An innocent person" is the figurative meaning of the word *lamb*. But to be an innocent person, you have to be falsely accused of something.

Jesus was falsely accused of blasphemy, and soldiers came and took him away to be crucified as if he were a thief: "Are ye come out as against a thief with swords and staves for to take me?" (Recorded in Matthew, Mark, and Luke). So Jesus said, "Fine, that is the way I will return. I will manifest my spirit in another innocent man that the Father chooses, that the wicked will slay, but I will raise him back up, even twice! I will even let 'they who pierce him' see his face to let them know that this is the one I and the father chose by making his vesture dipped in blood! (Rev. 3:20; John 6; Rev. 2:11; Rev. 1:7; Rev. 19:13).

"That'll show you! Oh, and I will give him the authority to judge you and the world as I said before: 'For the Father judges no man, but hath *committed all judgment unto the Son* [italics mine]. That all men should honor the Son, even as they honor the Father. He that honors not the Son honors not the Father, which hath sent him. For as the Father hath life in himself; so hath he given to the

Son to have life in himself; and hath given him authority to execute judgment also, because he is the Son of man'" (John 5:22–23, 26–27).

This life that is in the Son, which was given to him in God's will, is when Jesus's spirit came in to him when he opened the door when Jesus stood at the door and knocked in Revelation 3:20. Remember that God said "Vengeance is mine, I will repay?" well, now, vengeance is in the wrath of the lamb as written in these verses:

> For the great day of his wrath [the Lamb] is come; and who shall be able to stand? (Rev. 6:17)
> Out of his mouth goes a sharp sword, that with it he will smite the nations: and he shall rule them with a rod of iron: and he will tread the winepress of the fierceness and wrath of Almighty God. (Rev 19:15)

There you go. When you put the verses together that pertain to each other, you can really see the personality of the Father and the Son. He is a just God, and all of these things are written in his will and testament so when they are executed, the curse on the earth can be removed and there shall be no more evil and all of the other things that are of God that are written within shall be done. He came to earth by incarnating himself in Jesus and they killed him as said in these verses: "And without controversy great is the mystery of godliness: God was manifest in the flesh." (1 Tim. 3:16) and "Hereby perceive we the love of God, because he laid down his life for us" (1 John 3:16).

You have to love the irony of both of these verses being 3:16! And also notice what we learned earlier about the word *he* referring to the earlier subject in the sentence so that when this verse says "Because he laid down his life for us," it means "Because God laid down his life for us." So let us put an end to this controversy right here and now with even only these two scriptures.

The spirit of God was incarnated, made visible, and made manifest in the flesh of Jesus. Can you see the depths of Satan and his children how they would kill any man, let alone a man who obviously had a close connection with God and his power, who did so many healings and even brought the dead back to life, let alone Almighty God himself undercover? I mean, paint a picture in your mind of watching a man who was born not able to see and watching him grow up in your community as a blind child, then as a blind man, and then him coming across Jesus and telling him that he believed he could restore his sight, and then the next thing you know, you see him walking around able to see and telling people how Jesus just said to him his faith and belief in Jesus healed him. Then you hear people start to say "Kill him! He did work on the Sabbath!"

I would be like, "Hey, stupid, you can't see a single tree because the forest is blocking your view, can you? He just brought this guy's sight back to him today, and the other day he went to a guy who was dead for days and smelled like it, and the dead guy came back to life and was hanging out with his family again! I saw it with my own two eyes! You call yourself a priest of the Lord, and you want to kill a guy who demonstrated the power of God?"

Reincarnation

The wicked witnessed these things and refused to believe it because of their wickedness. They loved ruling their world of evil instead of the righteousness of God. These were the same people who were saying that Elias must come first before the messiah. Some people even said that Jesus was the reincarnation of Elias, and others thought one of the old prophets had risen again, and others thought he was John the Baptist reincarnated (Luke 9:19). This is recorded in the gospels of Matthew, Mark, and Luke.

The point here is that, way back then, they were all looking for Elias's spirit to return to earth in the flesh again. Today, this is what we call reincarnation. Have you ever heard of any Christian church that even mentions the word *reincarnation*, let alone believes that it exists? I think that you would be hard-pressed to find any church leader or teacher of the Bible to acknowledge that it is even possible, let alone a biblical fact. Well, let's turn to the words of the scripture and see what we can reveal about this matter of reincarnation.

In the first chapter of Luke, an angel announces the birth of John the Baptist to his mother and father, Elizabeth and Zacharias, and saying how great he will be in the sight of the Lord and will be filled with the Holy Ghost, even from his mother's womb, and then the angel said, "And he shall go before him *in the spirit and power of Elias*" (Luke 1:17; italics mine). Hidden in this verse, in plain sight, the angel is prophesying that the spirit and power of Elias is going to be in the child *from the womb* whom they are to call John, who becomes known as John the Baptist. When a spirit is made visible, or manifest, it's said to be incarnated in the flesh, to become human. When the same spirit is incarnated in the flesh again, it is called reincarnated, which is what we have here. Now, this is just an angel of the lord saying this, so people may dispute the words of an angel. But what does Jesus say about John?

Jesus said, "And from the days of John the Baptist until now the kingdom of heaven suffereth violence, and the violent take it by force" (Matt. 11:12). This is another little surprise that contradicts a lot of church teachings and proves them to be doctrines of men: we're already in the kingdom of heaven, but the violently wicked children of the devil are ruling it by force!

John, preparing the people to receive Jesus, was the first one to proclaim, "Repent ye: for the kingdom of heaven is at hand" (Matt. 3:2). When you have something at hand, like a wrench or a knife and fork at your dinner table, it is within your reach to grab it and use it. This is the exact same meaning of being able to take hold of the kingdom of heaven that you are standing in right now. What prevents this from happening are the keys of knowledge.

And then Jesus said, "For all the prophets and the law prophesied until John" (Matt. 11:13). This is a simple and straightforward statement with a huge implication: the prophets and the law told of a future kingdom to come by prophesying, or foretelling of a future event; and John proclaimed that, in fact, it was there at hand, *right then*, for the first time on earth.

And then finally, Jesus said, "And if ye will receive it, this is Elias, which was for to come" (Matt. 11:14). I love this little piece of hidden manna and the casual way that Jesus drops the bombshell that John the Baptist is the reincarnation of Elias! He kind of just slips it in like, "Oh yah, by the way, this Elias that you've been waiting and looking for, he was John whom they killed." And then continues talking about other stuff and the people don't even realize what he just said because a whole bunch of chapters later, his disciples asked him why the scribes say that Elias must come first.

So, in Matthew 17:11–13 the Bible says,

Jesus answered and said unto them, Elias truly shall first come, and restore all things. But I say unto you, that Elias is come already, and they knew him not, but have done unto him whatsoever they listed. Likewise shall also the Son of man suffer of them. Then the disciples understood that he spake [spoke] unto them of John the Baptist.

So far, this revelation of John the Baptist being the reincarnation of Elias was a pretty big bombshell, but now it's about to go nuclear: "*Likewise shall also the Son of man suffer of them*" (Matt. 17:12; italics mine).

Time to sit back and take a deep breath and let these words sink in. When Jesus returns by coming into the Son of man, they will treat the Son just like they treated Jesus and John and kill him without knowing who he is, but Jesus will give him life and raise him up so he shall never see death and shall not even be hurt of the second death (John 8:51 and Rev. 2:11). Isn't this a much simpler way for Christ to return rather than all the different fables and wild interpretations that all the different denominations of religions have to offer? The words have always been there in the scripture, only that every man is a liar and the word of God is the truth—the same exact words that have always been there now have new meaning. You see, before Jesus ascended back to heaven with his Father, even then he had to "open their understanding, that they might understand the scriptures" (Luke 24:45). Isn't it surprising to see that when God said he would make all things new again? He even makes the exact same words in the scripture new again with a different meaning.

Seeing through the clouds

Oh, the power of words. Within them is the power to create or destroy. They have the power to bring a blessing on a soul or to curse it. But how can the same words as in all of the scriptures that have been presented here thus far have such a different meaning than what we have learned as we grew up in the faith and belief in God? It is not the words themselves printed in the book or each their definitions written in the dictionary that have changed through the course of time; it is the men who are in the positions of leadership and authority whom everyone depends on to guide us to God.

I mean, since we all know that Satan is the ruler of this world that is sinking under the weight of all the lies and evil works, is it logical that we would have 100 percent godly men to instruct us on the truth of God? Or would the teachers of religion be Satan's top priority to put his servants in charge of leading God's innocent sheep astray? I think it would be the latter. I don't say this to be mean to the teachers of religion; I say this because we were forewarned of this many times and in a huge way. We all know that we are in the end-times with all the signs fulfilled, with the exception of the revelation of the Son, so take a little look at this small samplings of the warnings we were given:

> For the time will come when they will not endure sound doctrine; but after their own lusts shall they heap to themselves teachers, having itching ears;
> And they shall turn away their ears from the truth, and shall be turned unto fables. (2 Tim. 4:3–4)

> But there were false prophets also among the people, even as there shall be false teachers among you, who privily shall bring in damnable heresies, even denying the Lord that bought them, and bringing upon themselves swift destruction and many shall follow their pernicious ways; by reason of whom the way of truth shall be evil spoken of. (2 Pet. 2:1–2)

That we henceforth be no more children, tossed to and fro, and carried about with every wind of doctrine, by the sleight of men, and cunning craftiness, whereby they lie in wait to deceive. (Eph. 4:14)

Now the Spirit speaketh expressly, that in the latter times some shall depart from the faith, giving heed to seducing spirits, and doctrines of devils;
Speaking lies in hypocrisy; having their conscience seared with a hot iron. (1 Tim. 4:1–2)

All the devils disguised as the angels of the light have to do is have people believing that a "Super Jesus" will be flying around sucking people into the air as in their crazy rapture fable when he actually returns the same way as he came the first time: born of a woman.

And now we have a special bite of hidden manna in the following verses from 2 Timothy 2:17–18. See if you can apply the knowledge that you have acquired by reading this book so far and find a revelation, uncover something previously hidden in a shocking or surprising way:

And their word will eat as doth a canker: of whom is Hymenaeus and Philetus [they're just two guys]; Who concerning the truth have erred, saying that the resurrection is past already; and overthrow the faith of some.

<u>Do you see it? Okay, I will narrow it down a little bit for you.</u> Who, concerning the truth, have erred, saying that the resurrection is past already and overthrow the faith of some?

Okay, we have two guys that, concerning the truth of Jesus's gospel as it is revealed in this book you are reading now—which is that he will raise (resurrect) the Son as the Father did him—they're going around telling people a lie that the resurrection of the Son has already passed and causing people to lose their faith in the gospel. This writer couldn't be talking about the resurrection of the saints at the end of the world because that makes absolutely no sense and is not reasonable. I can't even think of a way to phrase a hypothetical question as an argument against that! Did all their ancestors already come back, even Abraham?

Sometimes, the hidden manna isn't in the meaning of the words but, rather, the clear understanding of the thought that the sentence is expressing. But you always have to remember that it is written as a mystery so the godly can see it plainly, as the common people heard him gladly, and it remains hidden to the wicked as said in the Bible:

> Unto you it is given to know the mystery of the kingdom of God: but unto them that are without, all these things are done in parables: That seeing they may see, and not perceive; and hearing they may hear, and not understand; lest at any time they should be converted, and their sins should be forgiven them. (Mark 4:11–12)

This shows us that the kingdom of God is not for everybody, and obviously, there are those that have their everlasting life in the lake of fire. But there are also a lot of people that have the mark of the beast that have a place in the kingdom:

> And I saw as it were a sea of glass mingled with fire: and them that had gotten the victory over the beast, and over his image, and over his mark, and over the number of his name, stand on the sea of glass, having the harps of God. (Rev. 15:2)

These are they who were converted in the end who were hoodwinked into accepting the mark of the beast and repented of their sin and no longer worship the image of the beast but worship God and the Lamb, the Son who shall make them free indeed of the beast. You see, in God's will and testament, the book of Revelation, it is God's will to cast them into the lake of fire:

> And the beast was taken, and with him the false prophet that wrought miracles before him, with which he deceived them that had received the mark of the beast, and them that worshipped his image. These both were cast alive into a lake of fire burning with brimstone. (Rev. 19:20)

This is where they are cast into the lake of fire, so this raises the obvious question of *If the beast and the false prophet are thrown into the lake and them that worshipped his image, how then can any of those who received the mark have a right to enter the kingdom of heaven?* This is another bite of hidden manna that requires reasoning. The mystery lies within the words *and them that worshipped his image.* This much we know that the ones who worship the image of the beast are cast into the lake of fire. But this raises a new question: What about the ones who have the mark of the beast and *don't* worship his image anymore because they have been converted, repent, and worship God and the Lamb? There you go, that's the other side of reason!

They are the ones who have the mark of the beast but whose sins were not worthy of eternal damnation and fire, so they are the workmen in the kingdom. After all, would your idea of heaven be working as a garbageman forever? I know that for the vast majority of us, that would not be much of a heaven; but for someone who has the mark of the beast because Satan hoodwinked them out of their crown of life, they will be filled with eternal bliss for having the privilege of picking up trash or stocking shelves at a grocery store or delivering mail or working at the sewage treatment plant forever! These are the ones "having the harps of God." They go around playing a beautiful musical instrument called a harp that God gave to them, forever.

Wait a minute, that sounds insanely stupid! I think that is what false teachers teach when they explain their fable of a rapture of his church of believers, somewhere floating in the sky when Jesus takes people out of the paradise of God here on earth where the kingdom of heaven resides! Like all the rest of words, there is more than one meaning, and in this verse, the word *harps* do not mean a stringed instrument. Have you ever had someone who always "harps" on you to do something? How about "When I go to my in-laws, my dad always 'harps' on me to get a job?" or how about "Will you stop 'harping' on me to get a haircut?"

Back to the kingdom of heaven and the ones who have the harps of God (they keep "harping" on everyone about how great God and the Lamb are), they are the ones who are the servants of God and the lamb forever as said in the Bible: "And there shall be no more curse: but the throne of God and of the Lamb shall be in it; *and his servants shall serve him*" (Rev. 22:3; italics mine).

They are also the ones who have to clean up everything that is evil and wicked in the paradise of God as the kingdom grows and

> the Son of man shall send forth his angels, and they shall gather out of his kingdom all things that offend, and them which do iniquity; And shall cast them into a furnace of fire: there shall be wailing and gnashing of teeth. Then shall the righteous shine forth as the sun in the kingdom of their father. Who hath ears to hear, let him hear" (Matt. 13:41–43).

After the angels take back the spirit of God, which gives people life, someone has to take care of the flesh until it returns to the dust from whence it came; and it is not the godly who have a crown of everlasting life charged with this task; it is the servants of the kingdom of God who are written in his will and testament. God did not leave anyone out of his will. The godly and the ungodly, the believer and the sorcerer, those who have the mark of the beast and worship his image, and those who have the mark and don't worship his image—everyone is included with a testament of what is to happen to them once God's will and testament is read. And by the way, what they call a furnace of fire back in the day, we would call a crematory or an incinerator today. This is what a furnace of fire is, compared to a lake of fire, which is lava.

Your *will* be done on earth as it is in heaven

We all know that the kingdom of heaven is like a mustard seed and it grows into a large tree where the birds come to lodge in its branches, and this is a figurative way of speaking as if I said to you at the beginning of building a skyscraper, "You can stand here on the street and watch it grow." Jesus used many parables to illustrate this growing and building of the kingdom of God, and one parable of which he revealed the meaning to his disciples told the exact way in which the kingdom comes. It is the parable of the wheat and tares found in Matthew 13.

This is where Jesus uttered things which have been kept secret from the foundation of the world. He tells us exactly how this world of evil that we are living in now passes away and the kingdom of God grows when the Son is revealed on earth. This explanation he gives us puts an end to all of the fables in religion that tell of the end of the world:

> He that soweth the good seed is the Son of man; The field is the world; the good seed are the children of the kingdom; but the tares are the children of the wicked one; The enemy that sowed them is the devil; the harvest is the *end of the world*; and the reapers are the angels. As therefore the tares [weeds] are gathered and burned in the fire; so *shall it be in the end of this world*. The Son of man shall send forth his angels, and they shall gather out of his kingdom all things that offend, and them which do iniquity; And shall cast them into a furnace of fire: there shall be wailing and gnashing of teeth. Then shall the righteous shine forth as the sun in the kingdom

of their Father. Who hath ears to hear, let him
hear. (Matt. 13:37–43; italics mine)

Jesus's revelation of how the end of the world makes sense, and
a child can even understand the simplicity of the coming of the end
of the world. Picture yourself as you are now in this wicked and evil
world, and the wicked abominable people start to simply disappear
because their spirit of life, which is God's, is taken from them by
the angels and they die; "and the young men arose, wound him up,
and carried him out, and buried him" (Acts 5:6), like Ananias and
Sapphira, his wife, in the book of Acts chapter 5.

People build the fable of a "church rapture" around twisting
half-truths of pieces of scripture. They take the part that says, "Two
men shall be in the field; the one shall be taken, and the other left"
(Mark 24:40; Luke 17:36), and say, "See, we get taken away into the
heavens in the sky!" What they won't put together with that scripture
is the one that follows it:

> And they answered and said unto him,
> Where, Lord? [Where do they go] And Jesus
> said unto them, Wheresoever the body is, thither
> (there) will the eagles be gathered together. (Luke
> 17:36–37)

Can you now see that he is saying that there will be two people
doing stuff and then the Son's angels takes back the spirit of life,
which is God's, of one of those people and then their body is taken
away and thrown to the buzzards, so to speak? And the other one is
left to shine forth in the kingdom as said in the Bible: "And the remnant were slain with the sword of him that sat upon the horse, which
sword proceeded out of his mouth: and all the fowls were filled with
their flesh" (Rev. 19:21).

This is one of the conditions of the race between God and
Satan, the battle of good and evil. The loser of the race has to clean
up the mess. Satan knows this because he has secretly raised his children to know how to do this cleaning as to not inconvenience the

children of God. The children of God have the crown of life and rule and reign in the kingdom of their father. (The word *rule* when used here, means that they are the most important people in the kingdom, kind of like a surfer or skateboarder would tell the best one among them "You rule, dude!") They are not the servants in the kingdom.

He also said how the wicked world will end in another parable of the net in Matthew 13:49–50:

> *So shall it be at the end of the world* [italics mine]: the angels shall come forth and sever the wicked from among the just, and shall cast them into the furnace of fire: there shall be wailing and gnashing of teeth.

How can you find a simpler way of explaining how the earth is cleansed of the evil things? The Son of God sends his angels to take back God's spirit of life from the children of the wicked one, which was on loan to them, and they will bury their own dead so the children of God can finally rule in the kingdom of God here on earth!

Remember, there are vessels of gold and vessels of clay, one is a vessel for honorable things and the other dishonor. This is similar to what we have here with the servants of the children of God in his kingdom as Jesus put in John 10:16: "And other sheep I have, which are not of this fold: them also I must bring, and they shall hear my voice; and there shall be one fold, and one shepherd." The other sheep, or people, who were not his and did not listen to his voice before will now listen to him manifest in the Lamb, thereby washing themselves clean by believing in the lamb of the book of Revelation:

> These are they which came out of great tribulation, and have washed their robes [wardrobes], and made them white in the blood of the Lamb. Therefore are they before the throne of God, *and serve him* day and night in his temple: and he that sitteth on the throne shall dwell among them. For the Lamb which is in the midst of the throne

shall feed them [shepherd them], and shall lead them unto living fountains of waters; and God shall wipe away all tears from their eyes. (Rev. 7:14–17; italics mine)

This also shows us that the lamb is revealed, or uncovered, on earth while the great tribulation is going on because these are the people who come out of the tribulation along with the children of God while it is happening. This is so perfectly stated by, of course, Jesus: "Watch ye therefore, and pray always, that ye may be accounted worthy to escape all these things that *shall* come to pass, *and to stand before the Son of man*" (Luke 21:36; italics mine). Just listen to the description of the end of this world and see if you can check off anything that has already happened:

But when ye shall hear of wars and commotions, be not terrified: for these things must first come to pass; but the end is not by and by. Nation shall rise against nation, and kingdom against kingdom: And great earthquakes shall be in diverse [various] places, and famines, and pestilences [fatal diseases]; and fearful sights and great signs shall there be from heaven. But before all these, they shall lay their hands on you, and persecute you, delivering you up to the synagogues, and into prison, being brought before kings and rulers for my name's sake. And it shall turn to you for a testimony. Settle it therefore in your hearts, not to meditate before what ye shall answer: For I will give you a mouth and wisdom, which all your adversaries shall not be able to gainsay nor resist. And ye shall be betrayed both by parents, and brethren, and kinsfolks, and friends; and some of you shall they cause to be put to death. And ye shall be hated of all men for my name's sake. But there shall not an hair of your head perish. In your patience possess ye your souls. And when ye shall see Jerusalem compassed with armies, then know that the desolation thereof is nigh [Jerusalem is utterly destroyed]. Then let them which are in Judaea flee to the mountains [Judaea is in the southern area of Palestine, where Israel is]; and let them which are in the midst of it depart out; and let not them that are in the countries enter thereinto. For these be the days of vengeance, that all things which are written may be fulfilled. But woe unto them that are with child, and to them that give suck, in those days! For there shall be great distress in the land, and wrath upon this people. And they shall fall by the edge of the sword, and shall be led away captive into all nations: and Jerusalem shall be trodden down of the Gentiles, until the times of the Gentiles be fulfilled.

And there shall be signs in the sun, and in the moon, and in the stars; and upon the earth distress of nations, with perplexity; the sea and the waves roaring [a lot of people coming in waves, screaming and yelling, protesting]; Men's hearts failing them for fear, and for looking after those things which are coming on the earth: for the powers of heaven shall be shaken. And then shall they see the Son of man coming in a cloud [cloud is figurative—meaning, "a state or cause of gloom"] with power and great glory. And when these things begin to come to pass, then look up, and lift up your heads; for your redemption draweth nigh. Behold the fig tree, and all the trees; When they now shoot forth, ye see and know of your own selves that summer is now nigh at hand. So likewise ye, when ye see these things come to pass, know ye that the kingdom of God is nigh at hand. Verily I say unto you, This generation shall not pass away, till all be fulfilled. Heaven and earth shall pass away [*pass*, as in "changing from one state or condition to another"; "into the new heaven and earth without a curse"]: but my words shall not pass away. And take heed to yourselves, lest at any time your hearts be overcharged with surfeiting, and drunkenness, and cares of this life, and so that day come upon you unawares. For as a snare shall it come on all them that dwell on the face of the whole earth. Watch ye therefore, and pray always, that ye may be accounted worthy to escape all these things that shall come to pass, and to stand before the Son of Man. (Luke 21:9–36; italics mine)

I think that everybody would agree that at least one or some of these things have come to pass or are happening presently. This should excite the believer because it says when these things *begin* to pass, we hold our head up for the son is about to be revealed. These things don't even have to actually fully happen because it says when they *begin* to happen. If it said "When these things happen," that would mean they would have to be fully executed, but it doesn't say that. When they *start* to happen, then pray that you are accounted worthy to stand before the Son so you can escape the things to come and come out of the mess that the world is about to experience and watch this evil world pass into the kingdom without a curse. The astrological events in the heavens mentioned here have been happening for a while, and most everyone dismisses them as simply normal and predictable ones—they have always happened.

The thing is, God created these signs in the heavens to turn us back to him and to live a godly life. It doesn't appear to me that this has worked too well with humanity. People just say "Wow, that was a cool-looking red moon, even after three in one year" or "Gee, that was one heck of a huge meteor over Russia, with all the damage that it caused" and what a beautiful solar eclipse followed with a lunar one. No one really stops to give God the credit for orchestrating these events to happen at a proper time in history millions of years in advance; we should, especially since all these events and their increased frequency add up to what we have here written in the book of Revelation.

Use these signs to discern the times that we are living in and live every day as if the Son will be the next breaking news story! I suppose that it does make sense that humanity should ignore these things so all of the words of God's will and testament should be fulfilled. I mean, how else can the whole world be caught unaware unless they ignore all of those signs set forth by God?

The son of perdition fulfills scripture

Now let us look even more carefully at the events preceding the revelation of the Son whom Jesus will raise in the last day. The second book of Thessalonians has a very good description of events that will compliment all of the things that have been revealed in the book you are reading right now. I always remember this book easily by calling it "2 Thess. 2." The Apostle Paul is writing to the Thessalonians for a second time to warn them not to be deceived by anyone concerning the return of Christ:

That ye be not soon shaken in mind, or be troubled, neither by spirit, nor by word, nor by letter as from us, as that the day of Christ is at hand.

Let no man deceive you by any means: for that day shall not come, except there come a falling away first, and that man of sin be revealed, the son of perdition. (2 Thess. 2:2–3)

First, the son of perdition has to be revealed. Is he revealed to everyone? No. He is revealed to the Son, the same as the first time with Jesus. Now we follow the trail in the scripture to find out who he is. Jesus mentions the son of perdition while he is praying for his disciples in John 17:12: "While I was with them in the world, I kept them in thy name: those that thou gavest me I have kept, and none of them is lost, but the son of perdition: that the scripture might be fulfilled."

Okay, we think we know who he is talking about, but we want to be sure of it. So let's keep looking deeper in scripture to find the hidden manna in the next verse that this refers us to in John 6:70: "Jesus told his Apostles, Have not I chosen you twelve, and one of you *is* [italics mine] a devil?" Now we know that he was speaking about Judas who was the one who betrayed him, and he said that he *is* a devil, but Paul cannot be talking about Judas in a letter written to the Thessalonians because Judas was long gone by then. So who is the son of perdition?

For this answer, we turn to John 13:27: "And after the sop Satan entered into him. Then said Jesus unto him, That thou doest, do quickly." Here we see a couple things. First, after Jesus dipped the bread and gave it to Judas, Satan entered into him; and second, this shows that the spirit of Satan himself can enter into a human being! This is what the son of perdition is: Satan incarnated in the flesh.

The son of perdition was the cause of Jesus being put to death by revealing his location so they could take him away secretly, by craft, without a crowd around the first time. And in the end, Satan incarnates himself again in a man, the son of perdition, who is revealed to the Son by causing him to be put to death as said in 2 Thessalonians 2:4: "Who opposeth and exalteth himself above all that is called God, or that is worshipped; so that he as God sitteth in the temple of God, showing himself that he is God."

The son of perdition is a very powerful sorcerer who uses the spirit of Satan himself. This is nothing new since Simon the sorcerer did this very same thing and used his sorcery to cast a spell on a whole city and had them believing that he was God and did the works of God:

**But there was a certain man, called
Simon, which beforetime in the same city used**

> **sorcery, and bewitched the people of Samaria, giving out that himself was some great one: To whom they all gave heed, from the least to the greatest, saying, this man is the great power of God. And to him they had regard, because that of long time he had bewitched them with sorceries. (Acts 8:9–11)**

> **Remember ye not, that, when I was yet with you, I told you these things? And now ye know what withholdeth that he might be revealed in his time.** For the mystery of iniquity doth already work: only he who now letteth will let, until he be taken out of the way. (2 Thess. 2:5–7)

The words *letteth will let* is like if I said "Let him be" and was saying "Leave him alone until he is taken out of the way."

The Bible says in 2 Thessalonians 2:8, "And then shall that Wicked be revealed, whom the Lord shall consume with the spirit of his mouth, and shall destroy with the brightness of his coming." This verse means that when the son of perdition is revealed to the Lord by fulfilling the word of God and slaying the innocent lamb in the fifth chapter of the book of Revelation, he is consumed by what he sees, which is Jesus raising him back to life right before his very eyes. Therefore, the breath of his mouth or the spirit still in his breath, which is life, is what consumes the wicked son of perdition. And then after that, the son of perdition is slowly destroyed by how happy and cheerful people become due to the fact that the Son has finally come, similar to saying to someone, "The brightness of her smile lit up the whole room!"

This is further revealed to us in the following verses:

> Even him, whose coming is after the workings of Satan with all power and signs and lying wonders,

> And with all deceivableness of unrighteous-
> ness in them that perish; because they received
> not the love of the truth, that they might be saved.
> The son of perdition and those that are with him
> do not love the truth, which is the fact that they
> just witnessed the innocent man they just mur-
> dered be resurrected by Jesus, thus fulfilling the
> prophecies written in the book of Revelation.
> And for this cause God shall send them
> strong delusions, that they should believe a lie:
> That they all might be damned who believed
> not the truth, but had pleasure in unrighteous-
> ness. (2 Thess. 2:9–12)

Now, any other person who is wicked or even half wicked would
probably instantly repent at the sight of murdering an innocent person and then watching God raise him back up minutes later from
the ground. But that is not meant for the son of perdition and his
servants. This is why God makes them delusional and lets them love
their lie to themselves, that the resurrection that happened before
their very eyes didn't happen, and then it slowly consumes them until
they are destroyed. The rest of the world will not know that this is
going on because these events take place at the time the spirit of
God/Jesus enters into the Son on earth. There is still more time and
other events that are written that must take place before the Son is
finally uncovered or, as it were, revealed.

The appearing of our Lord

Now the time has come to use the scripture to unveil the mystery of how the Son is revealed to everyone on earth, and it is not
how anyone expects it to be. But it is written in the Bible, and it
requires both the knowledge of the meanings of the words and common sense and reason to see the truth. It is found in the first letter, an

epistle, written by the apostle Paul to a man named Timothy. Read these verses in 1 Timothy 6:11–16 very carefully:

> But thou, O man of God, flee these things; and follow after righteousness, godliness, faith, love patience, meekness.
>
> Fight the good fight of faith, lay hold on eternal life, whereunto thou art also called, and hast professed a good profession before many witnesses.
>
> I give thee charge in the sight of God, who quickeneth (to make alive) all things, and before Christ Jesus, who before Pontius Pilate witnessed a good confession;
>
> That thou keep this commandment without spot, unrebukeable, until the appearing of our Lord Jesus Christ. (1 Tim. 6:11–14)

This is where the hidden manna is, right in the word *appearing*. This usage of the word is the second definition of the word *appear*, which means "seems" or "seems to be." It is the same sense used on your passenger-side rear-view mirror—objects in the mirror may be closer than they *appear*. This is saying that things in the mirror may be closer than they seem.

Another way to demonstrate this meaning of appearing is in this sample sentence: The guy went on stage *appearing* to be Elvis. This means, he seemed to look like him. This is what we have here in this verse—someone who looks and seems to be Jesus who will show us. And all we really know about what Jesus looks like is that he was a longhaired carpenter.

Let's continue on with the next verse:

> Which in his times he shall shew, who is the blessed and only Potentate, the King of kings, and Lord of lords. (1 Tim. 6:15)

This verse is loaded with a double whammy. On one hand, if you can't see the usage of the word *appearing* as aforementioned and still think that Jesus suddenly appears out of nowhere, then this verse says that Jesus will show us who the King of kings and Lord of lords is, which excludes himself, which is also true. On the other hand, what it actually says is someone who looks like Jesus will show us who the King of kings and Lord of lords is. The funny thing about the word *show* is that you have to have something in front of you to be able to show someone something. In this case, it is the Bible that is used to show who this one is, for it is written within God's will and testament exactly who the executor of his will is.

Let's continue reading on to the next verse:

> Who only hath immortality, dwelling in the
> light which no man can approach unto; whom
> no man hath seen, nor can see: to whom be hon-
> our and power everlasting. Amen. (1 Tim. 6:16)

He alone has immortality because only he was given to eat of the tree of life (read Revelation 2:7). And then, the word *light* has the meaning of "enlightenment"—as in, "do you see the light?" He has so much knowledge and enlightenment of God that no one can approach this understanding or has seen it or can see all of his knowledge for he is the Son of God.

After reading all of this, take some time to ponder, pray, and meditate on these things before you read the following chapters of the revelation of the revelation of St. John the Divine for it is a legally executable document ready to be executed. It couldn't be executed so far because all the names of the heirs have been concealed in mystery and lies of man's private interpretations of what the words mean. This is no longer the case since in this copy of God's will and testament, all the heirs are named. Everybody knows that in order for anyone's will to be read, you have to have all the heirs present to reveal what they inherit, and God's is no different. The time *is* at hand.

Revelation 1

The Revelation of the Revelation of St. John the Divine

The revelation of (by) Jesus Christ, which God gave unto him, to show unto his servants the things which must shortly come to pass, and he sent and signified it by his angel unto his servant John in the book of Revelation:

> Who bare record of the word of God, and of the testimony of Jesus Christ, and all things that he saw. Jesus is the angel that is showing John these things. Therefore, John keeps falling at his feet to worship him. John knows better than to do that to anyone other than Jesus. Remember, the man part of Jesus had his own spirit like you and I, and then when the spirit of God descended upon him and stayed, he became the host for the Lord of hosts to manifest in the flesh. This is proven later when he says, "I Jesus have sent mine angel to testify unto you these things".
>
> Blessed is he that readeth [*he* is singular, masculine; one person that reads with under-

standing the truth within], and they [plural, neutral gender] that hear [understand] the words of this *prophecy* [emphasis mine], and keep those things which are written therein: for the time is at hand.

John to the seven churches which are in Asia: Grace be unto you and peace, from him which is, and which was, and which is to come; and from the seven Spirits which are before his throne;

And from Jesus Christ, who is the faithful witness, and the first begotten of the dead [when Jesus says "I am the first and the last," this is what he means: the first and the last begotten of the dead. *Begotten* is the past participle of *beget*, which here means "to obtain." He was the first to obtain eternal life through death, and showed us how it's done], and the prince of the kings of the earth [prince, not king—the prince inherits the king's kingdom]. Unto him that loved us, and washed us from our sins in his own blood,

And hath made us kings and priests unto God and his Father; to him be glory and dominion for ever and ever. Amen.

Behold, he cometh with [accompanied by] clouds [the word *clouds* is figurative; vague, not clear; cause of trouble or worry; so he "comes with clouds of uncertainty," not floating in the sky]; and every eye shall see him [eventually], and they that pierced him [*they* is plural—meaning, "a small group of three or four." Jesus was pierced by one person; therefore, he is not speaking of himself; there is another]; and all kindred's of the earth shall wail because of him. Even so, Amen.

I am Alpha and Omega, the beginning and the ending [of the race], saith the Lord, which is, and which was, and which is to come, the Almighty [*the Almighty* is always in reference to God; Jesus says here that he is Almighty God speaking].

I John, who also am your brother, and companion in tribulation, and in the kingdom [he had the knowledge of the truth of the kingdom therefore was in it] and patience of Jesus Christ, was in the isle that is called Patmos, for the word of God, and for the testimony of Jesus Christ.

I was in the Spirit on the Lord's day, and heard behind me a great voice, as of a trumpet,

Saying, I am Alpha and Omega [every letter of the word of God], the first and the last [begotten of the dead]; and, What thou seest, write in a book, and send it unto the seven churches which are in Asia; unto Ephesus, and unto Smyrna, and unto Pergamos, and unto Thyatira, and unto Sardis, and unto Philadelphia, and unto Laodicea.

And I turned to see the voice that spake with me. And being turned, I saw seven golden candlesticks;

And in the midst of the seven candlesticks one like unto the Son of man, clothed with a garment down to the foot, and girt about the paps with a golden girdle.

His head and his hairs were white like wool, and white as snow; and his eyes were as a flame of fire [*flame of fire* is figurative—for example, do you remember your first flame that set your soul on fire? It is the emotions generated];

And his feet like unto fine brass, as if they burned in a furnace; and his voice as the sound of many waters.

And he had in his right hand seven stars: and out of his mouth went a sharp twoedged sword [words that cut like a knife]: and his countenance was as the sun shineth in his strength.

And when I saw him, I fell at his feet as dead [passed out]. And he laid his right hand upon me, saying unto me, Fear not; I am the first and the last [begotten of the dead]: I am he that liveth, and was dead; and, behold, I am alive for evermore, Amen; and have the keys [knowledge] of hell and of death.

Write the things which you hast seen, and the things which are, and the things which shall be hereafter;

The mystery of the seven stars which you sawest in my right hand, and the seven golden candlesticks. The seven stars are the angels of the seven churches: and the seven candlesticks which you sawest are the seven churches. (Rev. 1:2–20)

This is where the beginning of the mystery is: He already has the seven angels of the seven churches in his right hand, so why would he need John to write a letter to them? Because this is the beginning of making fools of the false preachers, pastors, and teachers! If a prophecy requires interpretation, the interpretation is always given shortly before or after. If the interpretation is not given, then it is not prophecy. It is God writing a mystery to make fools of the false teachers who consider themselves wise to expose them. What a cool God, eh?

Revelation 2

The letters to everyone

Let's continue omn to Revelation 2:

> Unto the angel of the church of Ephesus write; These things saith he that holdeth the seven stars in his right hand, who walketh in the midst of the seven golden candlesticks;
>
> I know thy works, and thy labour, and thy patience, and how thou canst not bear them which are evil: and you hast tried them which say they are apostles, and are not, and hast found them liars:
>
> And hast borne, and hast patience, and for my name's sake hast laboured, and hast not fainted.
>
> Nevertheless I have somewhat against thee, because thou hast left thy first love.
>
> Remember therefore from whence thou art fallen, and repent, and do the first works; or else I will come unto thee quickly, and will remove thy candlestick [church, as stated earlier] out of his place, except thou repent [except you repent

means that the aforementioned does not have to happen].

But this thou hast, that thou hatest the deeds of the Nicolaitanes, which I also hate.

He that hath an ear [everybody], let him hear [*hear* here is figurative for "let him understand"—as in, "do you *hear* what I'm saying?"] what the Spirit saith unto the churches [*churches* is plural, and like it says, it means all the churches—everyone and every church]; To him ["the one" male person] that overcometh will I give to eat of the tree of life, which is in the midst of the paradise of God. (Rev. 2:1–7)

This is the first of the ten verses Jesus gives what he has to the one who overcomes death as he also overcame death by resurrection by God. Here, he is giving the tree of life, which—according to Genesis 3:22 says, "And take also of the tree of life, and eat, and live forever"—is immortality, to live forever and not die. Jesus promised this to one person in John 8:51: "Verily, verily [truly, truly], I say unto you, if a [one] man keep my saying, he shall never see death." This does not mean he will live, die, and then live again in the resurrection of all souls; it means live and not die in the present, which is the lamb who was slain in chapter 5.

Let's proceed with the chapter.

And unto the angel of the church in Smyrna write; These things saith the first and the last, which was dead, and is alive;

I know thy works, and tribulation, and poverty, (but you are rich) and I know the blasphemy of them which say they are Jews, and are not, but are the synagogue of Satan.

Fear none of those things which thou shalt suffer: behold, the devil shall cast some of you into prison, that ye may be tried; and you shall have tribulation ten days: be you faithful unto death, and I will give thee a crown of life.

He that hath an ear [everyone], let him hear [understand] what the Spirit saith unto the churches [also plural, "all churches"]; He that overcometh shall not be hurt of the second death (This same one that he is prophesying about will overcome death as Jesus did, but twice].

And to the angel of the church in Pergamos write; These things saith he which hath the sharp sword with two edges;

I know thy works, and where thou dwellest, even where Satan's seat is: and thou holdest fast my name, and hast not denied my faith, even in those days wherein Antipas was my faithful martyr, who was slain among you, where Satan dwelleth [this shows that Satan has a seat of power in a different location than where he lives].

But I have a few things against thee, because thou hast there them that hold the doctrine of Balaam, who taught Balac to cast a stumbling-block before the children of Israel [Jacob], to eat things sacrificed unto idols, and to commit fornication.

So hast thou also them that hold the doctrine of the Nicolaitanes, which thing I hate.

Repent; or else I will come unto thee quickly, and will fight against them with the sword of my mouth [this is also echoed in Isaiah 11:4: "And with the breath of his lips shall he slay the wicked"].

He that hath an ear, let him hear what the Spirit saith unto the churches; To him that overcometh [the same man] will I give to eat of the hidden manna, and will give him a white stone, and in the stone a new name written, which no man knoweth saving he that receiveth it. (Rev. 2:8–17)

Jesus's words are the bread of life, so the hidden manna is the hidden meaning of his prophecies that are being revealed while you read this. The "white stone" is the Bible because, figuratively speaking, the word of God is written in stone and the pages are white. Note that he says "in" and not "on," which would be on the *outside* of the stone and not *in* the stone, and Jesus says he will give this new name to the one who overcomes. This is the one man that Jesus spoke of in John 6:50: "This is the bread which cometh down from heaven, that a [one] man may eat thereof, and not die."

> And unto the angel of the church in Thyatira write; These things saith the Son of God, who hath his eyes like unto a flame of fire, and his feet are like fine brass;
>
> I know thy works, and charity, and service, and faith, and thy patience, and thy works; and the last to be more than the first.
>
> Not withstanding I have a few things against thee, because thou sufferest that woman Jezebel, which calleth herself a prophetess, to teach and to seduce my servants to commit fornication, and to eat things sacrificed unto idols. (Rev. 2:18–20)

As we read in the preceding verses, Jesus spoke this in the book of Revelation, which means "prophecy," "telling a future event," and Jezebel lived way back in the books of Kings in the old testament! This means that her spirit and witchcraft is still an influence as written in 2 Kings 9:22: "And it came to pass, when Joram saw Jehu, that he said, Is it peace, Jehu? And he answered, What peace, so long as the whoredoms of thy mother Jezebel and her witchcrafts are so many?"

And I gave her space to repent of her fornication; and she repented not.

Behold, I will cast her into a bed, and them that commit adultery with her into great tribulation, except they repent of their deeds.

And I will kill her children with death; and all the churches shall know that I am he which searcheth the reins and hearts: and I will give unto every one of you according to your works.

But unto you I say, and unto the rest in Thyatira, as many as have not known the depths of Satan, as they speak; I will put upon you none other burden.

But that which ye have already hold fast till I come.

And he that overcometh [the same, one man who overcometh], and keepeth my works unto the end, to him [!] will I give power over the nations:

And he shall rule them with a rod of iron; as the vessels of a potter shall they be broken to shivers; even as I received of my Father.

And I will give him the morning star. (Rev. 2:21–28)

In the previous verses, specifically verses 26–28, Jesus says he will give to the one man who overcomes all the power he was given from his Father God, including himself as the morning star, which is the sun (the title *Son*), not Venus which is a planet.

He that hath an ear [everyone] let him hear [understand] what the Spirit saith unto the churches [again, *churches* is plural—meaning, "all churches and all people"]. (Rev. 2:29)

Revelation 3

The will

Now let's move on to Revelation 3.

And unto the angel of the church in Sardis write; These things saith he that hath the seven spirits of God, and the seven stars; I know thy works, that thou hast a name that thou livest, and art dead.

Be watchful, and strengthen the things which remain, that are ready to die: for I have not found thy works perfect before God.

Remember therefore how thou hast received and heard, and hold fast, and repent. If therefore thou shalt not watch, I will come on thee as a thief, and thou shalt not know what hour I will come upon thee.

Thou hast a few names even in Sardis which have not defiled their garmets; and they shall walk with me in white: for they are worthy.

He that overcometh [the same, one man], the same shall be clothed in white raiment; and I will not blot out his name out of the book of life, but I will confess his name before my Father, and before his angels. [Jesus says here that he will not blot out his name because he first gave him immortality in Revelation 2:7. He confesses his name to his Father that this is the chosen one.]

He that hath an ear, let him hear what the Spirit saith unto the churches [again, to everyone in every church].

And to the angel of the church in Philadelphia write; These things saith he that is holy, he that is true, he that hath the key of David, he that openeth, and no man shutteth; and shutteth, and no man openeth;

I know thy works: behold, I have set before thee an open door, and no man can shut it: for thou hast a little strength, and hast kept my word, and hast not denied my name.

Behold, I will make them of the synagogue of Satan, which say they are Jews, and are not, but do lie [the church leaders who are Satan's servants disguised as angels of the light]; behold, I will make them to come and worship before thy feet, and to know that I have loved thee.

Because thou hast kept the word of my patience, I also will keep thee from the hour of temptation, which shall come upon all the world to try them that dwell upon the earth.

Behold, I come quickly: hold that fast which thou hast, that no man take thy crown.

Him (the same one) that overcometh will I make a pillar [a *pillar* is a person regarded as reliably providing essential support for something—in this case, the word of God] in the temple of my God, and he shall go no more out; and I will write upon him the name of my God [God], and the name of the city of my God, which is new Jerusalem [which is not in the same geographic

location as the old Jerusalem, the same as England
is not in the same place as New England], which
cometh down out of heaven from my God: and I
will write upon him my new name. (Rev. 3:1–12)

In the preceding verse, Jesus's new name is the old name of the
overcomer and the new name of the one who overcomes Jesus said
he would write in the white stone (Revelation 2:17) will be revealed
later in this book. Remember, it is written that everyone that calls
upon the name of the Lord shall be saved? What is his new name to
call upon? Let's continue reading:

He that hath an ear, let him hear what the
Spirit saith unto the churches.
And unto the angel of the church of the
Laodiceans write; These things saith the Amen,
the faithful and true witness, the beginning of
the creation of God. (Rev. 3:13–14)

Surprise! This is a letter written to a people instead of a place.
Laodicea is a city. The word *Laodicean*, by definition, is one who is
indifferent or lukewarm, especially in religion. If it were written to
the people in Laodicea, it would say "in Laodicea," but it says "*of* the
Laodiceans."

I know thy works, that thou art neither
cold nor hot: I would thou wert cold or hot [see?
Lukewarm, indifferent].
So then because thou art lukewarm, and
neither cold, nor hot: I will spue thee out of my
mouth.
Because thou sayest, I am rich, and increased
with goods, and have need of nothing; and know-
est not that thou art wretched, and miserable,
and poor, and blind, and naked:

> I counsel thee to buy of me gold tried in the
> fire, that thou mayest be rich; and white raiment,
> that thou mayest be clothed, and that the shame
> of thy nakedness do not appear; and anoint thine
> eyes with eyesalve, that thou mayest see.
>
> As many as I love, I rebuke and chasten: be
> zealous therefore, and repent.
>
> Behold, I stand at the door [of your heart]
> and knock: if any [one] man hear my voice, and
> open the door, I will come in to him, and will sup
> with him, and he with me. (Rev. 3:15–20)

Notice he does not say "into him" but "in to *him*." This puts emphasis on *him*. This "him" is the same overcomer that he has given himself to, even the morning star. Jesus told his disciples in Matthew 17:12–13 that John the Baptist was the incarnation, or reincarnation, of Elias; and this is how the son of man would return:

> But I say unto you, That Elias is come
> already, and they knew him not, but have done
> unto him whatsoever they listed. Likewise shall
> also the Son of man suffer of them. Then the
> disciples understood that he spake unto them of
> John the Baptist. (Matt. 17:12–13)

John the Baptist was Elias who was to come first. He came back "undercover," and Jesus revealed to his disciples that he already came incarnated into John whom they killed. This is why Jesus, being a man, said that "no man knoweth the Son, but the Father; neither knoweth any man the Father, save [except] the Son, and to whomsoever the Son will reveal him" in Matthew 11:27. He also said this in Luke 10:22: "And no man knoweth who the Son is, but the Father; and who the Father is, but the Son, and he to whom the Son will reveal him [the Father]."

Yes, Jesus stood in front of his disciples and said no one knows who the Son is, which excludes himself, because he was there speaking, and they knew him. This mystery of the second son of God is hidden earlier in John 3:13 when Jesus says plainly, "And no man hath ascended up to heaven, but he that came down from heaven, even the *Son of man which is in heaven* [emphasis mine]." Jesus said this to his disciples, standing before them on earth, the Son he was speaking of was still in heaven at that time or hasn't been born of flesh yet.

Now, let's read the final two verses of Revelation 3:

> To him that overcometh (the same over-comer) will I grant to sit with me in my throne, even as I also overcame (the world, by resurrection of God), and am set down with my father in his throne. He that hath an ear, let him hear what the Spirit saith unto the churches [plural]. (Rev. 3:21–22)

This defines the overcomer in the book of Revelation. No one brought Jesus back to life but God. This is the prize of the race of life for one man: to sit with Jesus in the throne of God, which the word *throne* here is the position of power and authority, not a fancy seat. This is the reason for all the evil in the world. This is why every place of worship shall be destroyed because every so-called teacher in all churches lie about this second son to seek it for themselves—the devils, minions, synagogues of Satan. This is the prize for the race, and all races start with a rev up and a countdown as in Rev 3:21.

Revelation 4

The throne of God

After this I looked, and, behold, a door was opened in heaven: and the first voice which I heard was as it were of a trumpet talking with me; which said, Come up hither, and I will shew thee things which must be hereafter.

And immediately I was in the spirit: and, behold, a throne was set in heaven, and one sat on the throne.

And he that sat was to look upon like a jasper and a sardine stone: and there was a rainbow round about the throne, in sight like unto an emerald.

And round about the throne were four and twenty seats: and upon the seats I saw four and twenty elders sitting, clothed in white raiment; and they had on their heads crowns of gold.

And out of the throne proceeded lightnings and thunderings and voices: and there were seven lamps of fire burning before the throne, which are the seven Spirits of God. (Rev. 4:1–5)

In Revelation 4:1–5, see how the interpretation of prophecy is revealed in writing shortly after? The seven lamps are the seven spirits of God according to Isaiah 11:2: (1) the spirit of the Lord, (2) the spirit of wisdom, (3) the spirit of understanding, (4) the spirit of counsel, (5) the spirit of might (power), (6) the spirit of knowledge, and (7) the spirit of the fear of the Lord.

Let's move forward in Revelations 4.

> And before the throne there was a sea of glass like unto crystal: and in the midst of the throne, and round about the throne, were four beasts full of eyes before and behind.
>
> And the first beast was like a lion, and the second beast like a calf, and the third beast had a face as a man, and the fourth beast was like a flying eagle.
>
> And the four beasts had each of them six wings about him; and they were full of eyes within: and they rest not day and night, saying, Holy, holy, holy, Lord God Almighty, which was, and is and is to come. [These are the words of Jesus in Revelation 1:8: "Which is, and which was, and which is to come, the Almighty", so you know it is Jesus that sits on the throne of God.]
>
> And when those beasts give glory and honor and thanks to him that sat on the throne, who liveth for ever and ever,
>
> The four and twenty elders fall down before him that sat on the throne, and worship him that liveth for ever and ever, and cast their crowns before the throne, saying,
>
> Thou art worthy, O Lord, to receive glory and honour and power: for thou hast created all things, and for thy pleasure they are and were created. (Rev. 4:6–11)

Revelation 5

The second son

> And I saw in the right hand of him that sat
> on the throne [Jesus] a book written within and
> on the backside, sealed with seven seals.
> And I saw a strong angel proclaiming with a
> loud voice, Who is worthy to open the book, and
> to loose the seals thereof?
> And no man in heaven, nor in the earth,
> neither under the earth, was able to open the
> book, neither to look thereon.
> And I wept much, because no man was
> found worthy to open and to read the book, nei-
> ther to look thereon. (Rev. 5:1–4)

It says here in these verses, the book is the Bible read with the
understanding of the truth contained therein, as never has been
revealed before. They killed the people who knew the mystery of the
gospels, and so the lies began.

> And one of the elders saith unto me, Weep
> not: behold, the Lion (Lion is figurative, mean-
> ing a strong or courageous person) of the tribe of
> Juda, the Root of David, hath prevailed to open

the book and to loose the seven seals thereof.
(Rev. 5:5)

The lion who prevailed as referred here in verse 5 is the one who overcame as Jesus overcame in Revelation 3:21: "To him that overcometh will I grant to sit with me in my throne, *even as I also overcame* [emphasis mine], and am set down with my Father in his throne."

> And I beheld, and, lo, in the midst of the throne and of the four beasts, and in the midst of the elders, stood a Lamb as it had been slain, having seven horns and seven eyes, which are the seven Spirits of God sent forth into all the earth. (Rev. 5:6)

This lamb referred in verse 6 is the Son Jesus prophesied of in John 6:40:

> And this is the will of him that sent me [God], that every one which seeth the Son, and believeth on him [*him* refers to the masculine subject previously mentioned or easily recognized, which is referring to the Son], may have everlasting life: and I will raise him [the Son] up at the last day.

And again in John 6:44: "No man can come to me, except the Father which hath sent me draw [choose] him: and I will raise him [the son] up at the last day."

In John 6:50, Jesus shows the difference between everyone who believes in him who dies and will be resurrected, and the one whom the Father chooses who will not die, which is the Lamb in Revelation: "This is the bread which cometh down from heaven, that a man may eat thereof, *and not die* [emphasis mine]." And again in John 6:54:

Whoso [singular; "the one who"] eateth my
flesh [figurative for "digest his words"], and drin-
keth my blood [innocent as a lamb and slain like
him as said in Revelation 3:21], hath eternal life;
and I will raise him [singular] up at the last day.

And once again in John 6:58, Jesus explains the difference
between the resurrection of the dead and this one man he is talking
about, drawn to him by his Father:

This is that bread which came down from
heaven: not as your fathers did eat manna, *and
are dead, he* [the one, singular] that eateth of
this bread [digest his words] *shall live forever.*
(Emphasis added)

This is the root of the battle of good and evil, which Satan and
his children have been seeking, while all churches lie about this truth.
This is the race of life. Jesus was the first in the flesh to win and is the
last to win by his spirit coming in to the lamb or incarnating again in
the flesh. Jesus said this in many more places like John 8:51: "Verily,
verily, I say unto you, If a [one] man keep my sayings, he shall *never
see death* [emphasis mine]."

Let's further discuss the following verses in Revelation 5.

And he [the Lamb] came and took the book
out of the right hand of him [Jesus] that sat upon
the throne. (Rev. 5:7)

This is the verse that reveals the false teachers' biggest lie that
Jesus is the lion/lamb of the book of Revelation. How can Jesus be
this lamb and take the book out of his own right hand while he's
sitting on his throne? That is a stupid and obvious lie. What, does he
hold it in his right hand while he takes it with his left hand? That's
even more preposterous! Can you even picture that?

This verse is one of the biggest revelations of the truth all in itself. In John 1:29, John the Baptist stated, "Behold the Lamb of God, which taketh away the sin of the world." This is true! But the lamb here in Revelation is the one who "has redeemed us to our God" in the end of the world. God was incarnate in Jesus; so when he was crucified, he would leave the seven spirits of God sent forth in the earth.

> And when he had taken the book, the four beasts and four and twenty elders fell down before the Lamb, having every one of them harps, and golden vials full of odours, which are the prayers of saints.
> And they sung a new song, saying Thou art worthy to take the book, and to open the seals thereof: for thou was slain, and hast redeemed us to God by thy blood out of every kindred, and tongue, and people, and nation. (Rev. 5:8–9)

In these verses, Jesus's bloodline on his mother's side went to David, even to the root of David—his father, Jesse. Jesus's father's bloodline is God and has nothing to do with Joseph. Now, when it says "By thy blood out of every kindred, and tongue, and people, and nation," it is describing the mingled genetic pool that we have here today. By this description of "everyone's" blood, it also excludes him from being the Lamb.

Now let's read the final few verses of Revelation 5:

> And hast made us unto our God kings and priests: and we shall reign on the earth.
> And I beheld, and I heard the voice of many angels round about the throne and the beasts and the elders: and the number of them was ten thousand times ten thousand, and thousands of thousands;

Saying with a loud voice, Worthy is the Lamb that was slain to receive power, and riches, and wisdom, and strength, and honour, and glory, and blessing. [Jesus already had all of this, and now "raised it up in the last day."]

And every creature which is in heaven, and on the earth, and under the earth, and such as are in the sea, and all that are in them, heard I saying, Blessing and honour, and glory, and power, be unto him that sitteth upon the throne, and unto the Lamb for ever and ever.

And the four beasts said, Amen. And the four and twenty elders fell down and worshipped him that liveth for ever and ever. (Rev. 5:10–14)

Revelation 6

The four horsemen

And I saw when the Lamb opened one of the seals, and I heard, as it were the noise of thunder, one of the four beasts saying, Come and see.

And I saw, and behold a white horse: and he that sat on him had a bow; and a crown was given unto him: and he went forth conquering, and to conquer. [Couldn't this horseman go forth and conquer the other three horsemen?]

And when he had opened the second seal, I heard the second beast say, Come and see.

And there went out another horse that was red: and power was given to him that sat thereon to take peace from the earth, and that they should kill one another: and there was given unto him a great sword. (Rev. 6:1–4)

Revelation 6:1–4 is somewhat similar to Mark 13:8, which says,

For nation shall rise against nation, and kingdom against kingdom: and there shall be earthquakes in divers places, and there shall be famines and troubles: these are the beginnings of sorrows.

Have we not this presently? And in Mark 13:12 is the peace taken from the brotherhood that bear the mark of the beast when the families realize the parents hoodwinked the children out of their crown of life: "Now the brother shall betray the brother to death, and the father the son, and the children shall rise up against their parents, and shall cause them to be put to death." He doesn't say "The children shall kill the parents," but they will "cause them to be put to death."

> And when he had opened the third seal, I heard the third beast say, Come and see. And I beheld, and lo a black horse: and he that sat on him had a pair of balances in his hand.
> And I heard a voice in the midst of the four beasts say, A measure of wheat for a penny, and three measures of barley for a penny; and see thou hurt not the oil and the wine. (Rev 6:5–6)

Revelation 6:6 requires interpretation and none is given, so according to 2 Peter 1:20—"Knowing this first, that no prophecy of the scripture is of any private interpretation"—it does and should not have any interpretation.

Now, let's continue with Revelation 6's final verses:

> And when he had opened the fourth seal, I heard the voice of the fourth beast say, Come and see.
> And I looked, and behold a pale horse: and his name that sat on him was Death, and Hell followed with him. And power was given unto them over the fourth part of the earth, to kill with sword, and with hunger, and with death, and with the beasts of the earth.
> And when he had opened the fifth seal, I saw under the altar the souls of them that were slain for the word of God, and for the testimony which they held:

And they cried with a loud voice, saying, How long, O Lord, holy and true, dost thou not judge and avenge our blood on them that dwell on the earth?

And white robes were given unto every one of them; and it was said unto them, that they should rest yet for a little season, until their fellowservants also and their brethren, that should be killed as they were, should be fulfilled.

And I beheld when he had opened the sixth seal, and lo, there was a great earthquake; and the sun became black as sackcloth of hair [a total solar eclipse], and the moon became as blood [as all the recent blood moons];

And the stars of heaven fell unto the earth [The meteor showers and even the huge one of biblical proportion that was over Russia. These prophecies do not say they happen all at once, but "in those days" is what Jesus said about the end-times.], even as a fig tree casteth her untimely figs, when she is shaken of a mighty wind.

And the heaven departed as a scroll when it is rolled together [that's as simple as the clouds giving way to a clear sky]; and every mountain and island were moved out of their places.

And the kings of the earth, and the great men [leaders], and the rich men, and the chief captains, and the mighty men, and every bondman, and every free man, hid themselves in the dens and in the rocks of the mountains;

And said to the mountains and rocks, Fall on us, and hide us from the face of him that sitteth on the throne, and from the wrath of the Lamb:

For the great day of his wrath has come; and who shall be able to stand? (Rev. 6:7–17)

Revelation 7

Those who watch the great tribulation

And after these things I saw four angels standing on the four corners of the earth, holding the four winds of the earth, that the wind should not blow on the earth, nor on the sea, nor on any tree.

And I saw another angel ascending from the east, having the seal of the living God: and he cried with a loud voice to the four angels, to whom it was given to hurt the earth and the sea,

Saying, Hurt not the earth, neither the sea, nor the trees, till we have sealed the servants of our God in their foreheads.

And I heard the number of them which were sealed: and there were sealed an hundred and forty and four thousand of all the tribes of the children of Israel. (Rev. 7:1–4)

In these verses, Israel is always referring to Jacob and his children and his sons or descendants. The very first time Israel is mentioned in the Bible is in Genesis 32:28: "And he said [God], Thy name shall be called no more Jacob, but Israel: for as a prince hast thou power with God and with men, and hast prevailed."

It is the Hebrew nation or people descending from Jacob, not land or a place. The literal Hebrew meaning of *Israel* is "he that strives with God." The Jews, which is a religion—which are also Hebrews, a nationality of people from Hebron which is a city in Palestine and descendents of Jacob—occupy Palestine and call it the Jewish state of Israel, which is not recognized as a state by the United Nations. It is the biggest hoax in the world.

> Of the tribe of Juda were sealed twelve thousand. Of the tribe of Reuben were sealed twelve thousand. Of the tribe of Gad were sealed twelve thousand.
>
> Of the tribe of Aser were sealed twelve thousand. Of the tribe of Bepthalim were sealed twelve thousand. Of the tribe of Manasses were sealed twelve thousand.
>
> Of the tribe of Simeon were sealed twelve thousand. Of the tribe of Levi were sealed twelve thousand. Of the tribe of Issachar were sealed twelve thousand.
>
> Of the tribe of Zabulon were sealed twelve thousand. Of the tribe of Joseph were sealed twelve thousand. Of the tribe of Benjamin were sealed twelve thousand.
>
> After this I beheld, and, lo, a great multitude, which no man could number, of all the nations and kindreds, and people, and tongues, stood before the throne, and before the Lamb, clothed with white robes, and palms in their hands. (Rev. 7:5–9)

Can you see the comparison of a measly 144,000 direct descendants of Jacob (who God renamed Israel) to an innumerable number of people of all the nations, kindreds, people, and tongues? And palms were given out as a sign of victory, according to the dictionary.

> And cried with a loud voice, saying, Salvation to our God which sitteth upon the throne, and unto the Lamb.
>
> And all the angels stood round about the throne, and about the elders and the four beasts, and fell before the throne on their faces, and worshipped God,
>
> Saying, Amen: Blessing and glory, and wisdom, and thanksgiving, and honour, and power, and might, be unto our God for ever and ever. Amen.
>
> And one of the elders answered, saying unto me, What are these which are arrayed in white robes? And whence came they?
>
> And I said unto him, Sir, thou knowest. And he said to me, These are they which came out of great tribulation, and have washed their robes, and made them white in the blood of the Lamb. (Rev. 7:10–14)

Remember this Lamb in these verses is the overcomer of Revelation 2 and 3 in which the Spirit of Jesus came into or incarnated into as said in Revelation 3:20. This is the Son he said he would raise in John 6, and when Jesus was prophesying the end of the world he said,

> Watch ye therefore, and pray always, that ye may be accounted worthy to escape all these things that shall come to pass [*shall* is future tense], and to stand before the Son of man. (Luke 21:36)

Remember that the Son is on the earth when all these things "*begin* [emphasis mine] to come to pass" as said in Luke 21:28

Read on what is said in the final few verses of Revelation 7:

> Therefore are they before the throne of God, and serve him day and night in his temple: and he that sitteth on the throne shall dwell among them.
>
> They shall hunger no more, neither thirst any more; neither shall the sun light on them, nor any heat.
>
> For the Lamb which is in the midst of the throne shall feed them, and shall lead them unto living fountains of waters: and God shall wipe away all tears from their eyes. (Rev. 7:15–17)

Revelation 8

Not a pretty vision

Now let's read what happens next in Revelation 8.

> And when he had opened the seventh seal, there was silence in heaven about the space of half an hour.
>
> And I saw the seven angels which stood before God and to them were given seven trumpets.
>
> And another angel came and stood at the altar, having a golden censer; and there was given unto him much incense, that he should offer it with the prayers of all saints upon the golden altar which was before the throne.
>
> And the smoke of the incense, which came with the prayers of the saints, ascended up before God out of the angel's hand.
>
> And the angel took the censer, and filled it with fire of the altar, and cast it into the earth: and there were voices, and thunderings, and lightnings, and an earthquake.
>
> And the seven angels which had the seven trumpets prepared themselves to sound. [This is all just describing what he saw in the vision.]

The first angel sounded, and there followed hail and fire mingled with blood, and they were cast upon the earth: and the third part of trees was burnt up, and all green grass was burnt up.

And the second angel sounded, and as it were a great mountain burning with fire was cast into the sea: and the third part of the sea became blood;

And the third part of the creatures which were in the sea, and had life, died; and the third part of the ships were destroyed.

And the third angel sounded, and there fell a great star from heaven, burning as it were a lamp, and it fell upon the third part of the rivers, and upon the fountains of waters;

And the name of the star is called wormwood: and the third part of the waters became wormwood; and many men died of the waters, because they [the many men] were made bitter. [Yes, wormwood is a bitter plant; but here, the figurative meaning is a "state or source of bitterness or grief," which is what made them die.]

And the fourth angel sounded, and the third part of the sun was smitten, and the third part of the moon, and the third part of the stars; so as the third part of them was darkened, and the day shone not for a third part of it, and the night likewise.

And I beheld, and heard an angel flying through the midst of heaven, saying with a loud voice, Woe, woe, woe, to the inhabiters of the earth by reason of the other voices of the trumpet of the three angels, which are yet to sound! (Rev. 8:1–13)

Revelation 9

Bad day for sorcery

Let's see what happens next in Revelation 9.

>   And the fifth angel sounded, and I saw a star fall from heaven unto the earth: and to him was given the key of the bottomless pit.
>
>   And he opened the bottomless pit; and there arose a smoke out of the pit, as the smoke of a great furnace; and the sun and the air were darkened by reason of the smoke of the pit.
>
>   And there came out of the smoke locusts upon the earth: and unto them was given power, as the scorpions of the earth have power.
>
>   And it was commanded them that they should not hurt the grass of the earth, neither any green thing, neither any tree; but only those men which have not the seal of God in their foreheads.
>
>   And to them it was given that they should not kill them, but that they should be tormented five months: and their torment was as the torment of a scorpion, when he striketh a man.

And in those days shall men seek death, and shall not find it; and shall desire to die, and death shall flee from them.

And the shapes of the locusts were like unto horses prepared unto battle; and on their heads were as it were crowns like gold, and their faces were as the faces of men.

And they had hair as the hair of women, and their teeth were as the teeth of lions.

And they had breastplates, as it were breastplates of iron; and the sound of their wings was as the sound of chariots of many horses running to battle.

And they had tails like unto scorpions, and there were stings in their tails: and their power was to hurt men five months.

And they had a king over them, which is the angel of the bottomless pit, whose name in the Hebrew tongue is Abaddon [a name for the devil or for hell], but in the Greek tongue hath his name Apollyon [another name for the devil].

One woe is past; and, behold, there come two woes more hereafter.

And the sixth angel sounded, and I heard a voice from the four horns of the golden altar which is before God,

Saying to the sixth angel which had the trumphet, Loose the four angels which are bound in the great river Euphrates.

And the four angels were loosed, which were prepared for an hour, and a day, and a month, and a year, for to slay the third part of men.

And the number of the army of the horsemen were two hundred thousand thousand: and I heard the number of them.

And thus I saw the horses in the vision, and them that sat on them, having breastplates of fire, and of jacinth, and brimstone: and the heads of the horses were as the heads of lions; and out of their mouths issued fire and smoke and brimstone.

By these three was the third part of men killed, by the fire, and by the smoke, and by the brimstone, which issued out of their mouths [no interpretation—it's just what he saw].

For their power is in their mouth, and in their tails: for their tails were like unto serpents, and had heads, and with them they do hurt.

And the rest of the men which were not killed by these plagues yet repented not of the works of their hands, that they should not worship devils, and idols of gold, and silver, and brass, and stone, and of wood: which neither can see, nor hear, nor walk:

Neither repented they of their murders, nor of their sorceries, nor of their fornication, nor of their thefts. (Rev. 9:1–21)

Revelation 9:20–21 all has to do with sorceries. This is the main reason for the end of the world as you shall read later.

Revelation 10

Mystery of God to be declared

Revelation 10 holds an important message, even though this is considered a short chapter.

> And I saw another mighty angel come down from heaven, clothed with a cloud: and a rainbow was upon his head, and his face was as it were the sun, and his feet as pillars of fire:
> And he had in his hand a little book open: and he set his right foot upon the sea, and his left foot on the earth,
> And cried with a loud voice, as when a lion roareth: and when he had cried, seven thunders uttered their voices.
> And when the seven thunders had uttered their voices, I was about to write: and I heard a voice from heaven saying unto me, Seal up those things which the seven thunders uttered, and write them not.
> And the angel which I saw stand upon the sea and upon the earth lifted up his hand to heaven,

And sware by him that liveth for ever and ever, who created heaven, and the things that therein are, and the earth, and the things that therein are, and the sea, and the things which are therein, that there should be time no longer:

But in the days of the voice of the seventh angel, when he shall begin to sound, the mystery of God should be finished, as he hath declared to his servants the prophets,

And the voice which I heard from heaven spake unto me again, and said, Go and take the little book which is open in the hand of the angel which standeth upon the sea and upon the earth.

And I went unto the angel, and said unto him, Give me the little book. And he said unto me, Take it, and eat it up; and it shall make thy belly bitter, but it shall be in thy mouth sweet as honey.

And I took the little book out of the angel's hand, and ate it up; and it was in my mouth sweet as honey: and as soon as I had eaten it, my belly was bitter.

And he said unto me, Thou must prophesy again before many peoples, and nations, and tongues, and kings. (Rev. 10:1–11)

If it weren't for filler parts that aren't prophecy, the book of Revelation would be really short, so things like Revelation 10:8–11 are added to see what fools will try to interpret.

Revelation 11

Thy wrath is come

And there was given me a reed like unto a rod: and the angel stood, saying, Rise, and measure the temple of God, and the altar, and them that worship therein.

But the court which is without the temple leave out, and measure it not; for it is given unto the Gentiles: and the holy city shall they tread under foot forty and two months.

And I will give power unto my two witnesses, and they shall prophesy a thousand two hundred and threescore days, clothed in sackcloth.

These are the two olive trees, and the two candlesticks standing before the God of the earth.

And if any man will hurt them, fire proceedeth out of their mouth, and devoureth their enemies: and if any man will hurt them, he must in this manner be killed.

These have power to shut heaven, that it rain not in the days of their prophecy: and have power over waters to turn them to blood, and to smite the earth with all plagues, as often as they will.

> And when they shall have finished their testimony, the beast that ascendeth out of the bottomless pit shall make war against them, and shall overcome them, and kill them.
>
> And their dead bodies shall lie in the street of the great city, which spiritually is called Sodom and Egypt, where also our Lord was crucified. (Rev. 11:1–8)

Revelation 11:1–8 discusses Sodom and Egypt. The word *and* connects the two. Is Sodom in Egypt? No. In ancient history, it is somewhere in ancient Palestine, south of the Dead Sea. As best as they can guess, Sodom is nowhere close to Egypt. Was our Lord crucified in Egypt? No. This is more "filler" and is not prophecy but, rather, put in place to make fools of those who consider themselves wise.

> And they of the people and kindreds and tongues and nations shall see their dead bodies three days and an half, and shall not suffer their dead bodies to be put in graves.
>
> And they that dwell upon the earth shall rejoice over them, and make merry, and shall send gifts one to another; because these two prophets tormented them that dwelt on the earth.
>
> And after three days and an half the Spirit of life from God entered into them, and they stood upon their feet; and great fear fell upon them which saw them.
>
> And they heard a great voice from heaven saying unto them, Come up hither. And they ascended up to heaven in a cloud; and their enemies beheld them.
>
> And the same hour was there a great earthquake, and the tenth part of the city fell, and in the earthquake were slain of men seven thousand:

> and the remnant were affrighted, and gave glory
> to the God of heaven.
>
> The second woe is past; and, behold, the
> third woe cometh quickly.
>
> And the seventh angel sounded; and there
> were great voices in heaven, saying, The king-
> doms of this world are become the kingdoms of
> our Lord and of his Christ; and he shall reign for
> ever and ever. (Rev. 11:9–15)

This is in reference to Jesus, since in the next verse God is used and the following, "Lord God Almighty" is used. But we already know the two are one by Revelation 1:8 because it says the "Lord, which is, and which was, and which is to come, the Almighty [God]" (this Christ is the Lamb, the one who overcame, and Jesus wrote his new name upon in Revelation 3:12). Notice the Lord and of his Christ is plural—two people. But *he* is singular where it says "He shall reign forever." This is because Jesus said he (his spirit) would come in to the one who overcomes as he also overcame and grant to him to sit in his throne as he is sat down in his father's throne in Revelation 3:20–21.

Let's continue to see what this chapter holds for us.

> And the four and twenty elders, which sat
> before God on their seats, fell upon their faces,
> and worshipped God,
>
> Saying, We give thee thanks, O Lord God
> Almighty, which art, and wast, and art to come;
> because you hast taken to thee thy great power,
> and hast reigned.
>
> And the nations were angry, and thy wrath
> is come, and the time of the dead, that they
> should be judged, and that thou shouldest give
> reward unto thy servants the prophets, and to the
> saints, and them that fear thy name, small and

great; and shouldest destroy them which destroy the earth.

And the temple of God was opened in heaven, and there was seen in his temple the ark of his testament: and there were lightnings, and voices, and thunderings, and an earthquake, and great hail. (Rev. 11:16–19)

Revelation 12

The kingdom is coming

Revelation 12 is as straightforward as it is, with little to no interpretation. Read on to know what this chapter holds for us.

> And there appeared a great wonder in heaven; a woman clothed with the sun, and the moon under her feet, and upon her head a crown of twelve stars [where is the interpretation?]:
>
> And she being with child cried, travailing in birth, and pained to be delivered.
>
> And there appeared another wonder in heaven; and behold a great red dragon, having seven heads and ten horns, and seven crowns upon his heads [interpretation?].
>
> And his tail drew the third part of the stars of heaven, and did cast them to the earth: and the dragon stood before the woman which was ready to be delivered, for to devour her child as soon as it was born.
>
> And she brought forth a man child, who was to rule all nations with a rod of iron: and her child was caught up unto God, and to his throne.

And the woman fled into the wilderness, where she hath a place prepared of God, that they should feed her there a thousand two hundred and threescore days.

And there was war in heaven: Michael and his angels fought against the dragon; and the dragon fought and his angels,

And prevailed not; neither was their place found any more in heaven.

And the great dragon was cast out, that old serpent, called the Devil, and Satan, which deceiveth the whole world: he was cast out into the earth, and his angels were cast out with him. [Didn't Jesus say he saw this in Luke 10:18—"I beheld Satan as lightning fall from heaven"?]

And I heard a loud voice saying in heaven, Now is come salvation, and strength, and the kingdoms of our God, and the power of his Christ: for the accuser of our bretheren is cast down, which accused them before our God day and night.

And they overcame him by the blood of the Lamb [this is the Lamb in Revelation 7:14], and by the word of their testimony; and they loved not their lives unto the death.

Therefore rejoice, ye heavens, and ye that dwell in them. Woe to the inhabiters of the earth and of the sea! For the devil is come down unto you, having great wrath, because he knoweth that he hath but a short time.

And when the dragon saw that he was cast unto the earth, he persecuted the woman which brought forth the man child.

And to the woman were given two wings of a great eagle, that she might fly into the wilderness [she already fled into the wilderness in verse 6, didn't she?], into her place, where she is nourished for a time, and times, and half a time, from the face of the serpent,

And the serpent cast out of his mouth water as a flood after the woman, that he might cause her to be carried away of the flood.

And the earth helped the woman, and the earth opened her mouth, and swallowed up the flood which the dragon cast out of his mouth [no interpretation].

And the dragon was wroth with the woman, and went to make war with the remnant of her seed, which keep the commandments of God, and have the testimony of Jesus Christ. (Rev. 12:1–17)

Revelation 13

The patience of the saints

And I stood upon the sand of the sea, and saw
a beast rise up out of the sea, having seven heads
and ten horns, and upon his horns ten crowns,
and upon his heads the name of blasphemy.

And the beast which I saw was like unto a
leopard, and his feet were as the feet of a bear,
and his mouth as the mouth of a lion: and the
dragon gave him his power, and his seat, and
great authority.

And I saw one of his heads as it were
wounded to death; and his deadly wound was
healed: and all the world wondered after the
beast.

And they worshipped the dragon which gave
power unto the beast: and they worshipped the
beast, saying, Who is like unto the beast? Who is
able to make war with him? (Rev. 13:1–4)

We know who the dragon is because he is interpreted in
Revelation 12:9: "And the great dragon was cast out, that old serpent,
called the Devil, and Satan, which deceiveth the whole world." So
Revelation 13:4 is saying they worshipped the devil.

Let's read further what is said in this chapter.

> And there was given unto him a mouth speaking great things and blasphemies; and power was given unto him to continue forty and two months.
>
> And he opened his mouth in blasphemy against God, to blaspheme his name, and his tabernacle, and them that dwell in heaven.
>
> And it was given unto him to make war with the saints, and to overcome them: and power was given him over all kindreds, and tongues, and nations.
>
> And all that dwell upon the earth shall worship him, whose names are not written in the book of life of the lamb slain from the foundation of the world.
>
> If any man have an ear, let him hear.
>
> He that leadeth into captivity shall go into captivity: he that killeth with the sword must be killed with the sword. Here is the patience and the faith of the saints.
>
> And I beheld another beast coming up out of the earth; and he had two horns like a lamb, and he spake as a dragon.
>
> And he exerciseth all the power of the first beast before him, and causeth the earth and them which dwell therein to worship the first beast, whose deadly wound was healed.
>
> And he doeth great wonders, so that he maketh fire come down from heaven on the earth in the sight of men,
>
> And deceiveth them that dwell on the earth by the means of those miracles which he had power to do in the sight of the beast; saying to them that dwell of the earth, that they should

make an image to the beast, which had the wound by a sword, and did live.

And he had power to give life unto the image of the beast, that the image of the beast should both speak, and cause that as many as would not worship the image of the beast should be killed.

And he causeth all, both small and great, rich and poor, free and bond, to receive a mark in their right hand, or in their foreheads:

And that no man might buy or sell, save he that had the mark, or the name of the beast, or the number of his name.

Here is wisdom. Let him that hath understanding count the number of the beast: for it is the number of a man; and his number is Six hundred threescore and six. (Rev. 13:5–18)

Revelation 14

The harvest

And I looked, and, lo, a lamb stood on the mount Sion, and with him an hundred forty and four thousand, having his father's name written in their foreheads. [This is the Lamb in Revelation 5:6.]

And I heard a voice from heaven, as the voice of many waters, and as the voice of a great thunder: and I heard the voice of harpers harping with their harps:

And they sung as it were a new song before the throne, and before the four beasts, and the elders: and no man could learn that song but the hundred and forty and four thousand, which were redeemed from the earth.

These are they which were not defiled with women; for they are virgins. These are they which follow the Lamb whithersoever he goeth. These were redeemed from among men, being the first fruits unto God and to the Lamb.

And in their mouth was found no guile: for they are without fault before the throne of God.

And I saw another angel fly in the midst of heaven, having the everlasting gospel to preach unto them that dwell on the earth, and to every nation, and kindred, and tongue, and people,

Saying with a loud voice, Fear God, and give glory to him; for the hour of his judgment is come: and worship him that made heaven, and earth, and the sea, and the fountains of waters.

And there followed another angel, saying, Babylon is fallen, is fallen, that great city, because she made all nations drink of the wine of the wrath of her fornications.

And the third angel followed them, saying with a loud voice, If any man worship the beast and his image, and receive his mark in his forehead, or in his hand,

The same shall drink of the wine of the wrath of God, which is poured out without mixture unto the cup of his indignation; and he shall be tormented with fire and brimstone in the presence of the holy angels, and in the presence of the Lamb:

And the smoke of their torment ascendeth up for ever and ever: and they have no rest day or night, who worship the beast and his image, and whosoever receiveth the mark of his name.

Here is the patience of the saints: here are they that keep the commandments of God, and the faith of Jesus.

And I heard a voice from heaven saying unto me, Write, Blessed are the dead which die in the Lord from henceforth: Yea, saith the Spirit, that they may rest from their labours; and their works do follow them.

And I looked, and behold a white cloud, and upon the cloud one sat like unto the Son of

man, having on his head a golden crown, and in
his hand a sharp sickle. (Rev. 14:1–14)

In Revelation 14:14, if it said here on his head a "crown of gold," he would have a crown made of gold. However, it says "golden crown," which turns it into the figurative meaning of crown, which means, by definition, "a person's hair."

Continue reading what it says in this chapter's final few verses.

> And another angel came out of the temple, crying with a loud voice to him that sat on the cloud, Trust in thy sickle, and reap: for the time is come for thee to reap; for the harvest of the earth is ripe.
>
> And he that sat on the cloud thrust in his sickle on the earth; and the earth was reaped.
>
> And another angel came out of the temple which is in heaven, he also having a sharp sickle.
>
> And another angel came out from the altar, which had power over fire; and cried with a loud cry to him that had the sharp sickle, saying, Thrust in thy sharp sickle, and gather the cluster of the vine of the earth; for her grapes are fully ripe.
>
> And the angel thrust in his sickle into the earth, and gathered the vine of the earth, and cast it into the great winepress of the wrath of God.
>
> And the winepress was trodden without the city, and blood came out of the winepress, even unto the horse bridles, by the space of a thousand and six hundred furlongs. (Rev. 14:15–20)

Revelation 15

Preparing the way

And I saw another sign in heaven, great and marvelous, seven angels having the seven last plagues; for in them is filled up the wrath of God.

And I saw as it were a sea of glass mingled with fire: and them that had gotten the victory over the beast, and over his image, and over his mark, and over the number of his name, stand on the sea of glass, having the harps of God.

And they sing the song of Moses the servant of God, and the song of the Lamb, saying, Great and marvelous are thy works, Lord God Almighty; just and true are thy ways, thou King of saints.

Who shall not fear thee, O Lord, and glorify thy name? For thou only art holy: for all nations shall come and worship before thee; for thy judgments are made manifest.

And after that I looked, and, behold, the temple of the tabernacle of the testimony in heaven was opened:

And the seven angels came out of the temple, having the seven plagues, clothed in pure and white linen, and having their breasts girded with golden girdles.

And one of the four beasts gave unto the seven angels seven golden vials full of the wrath of God, who liveth for ever and ever.

And the temple was filled with smoke from the glory of God, and from his power; and no man was able to enter into the temple, till the seven plagues of the seven angels were fulfilled. Rev. 15:1–8)

Revelation 16

True and righteous judgments

And I heard a great voice out of the temple saying to the seven angels, Go your ways, and pour out the vials of the wrath of God upon the earth.

And the first went, and poured out his vial upon the earth; and there fell a noisome and grievous sore upon the men which had the mark of the beast, and upon them which worshipped his image.

And the second angel poured out his vial upon the sea; and it became as the blood of a dead man: and every living soul died in the sea.

And the third angel poured out his vial upon the rivers and foundations of waters; and they became blood.

And I heard the angel of the waters say, Thou art righteous, O Lord, which art, and wast, and shalt be, because thou hast judged thus.

For they have shed the blood of saints and prophets, and thou hast given them blood to drink; for they are worthy.

And I heard another out of the altar say, Even so, Lord God Almighty, true and righteous are thy judgments.

And the fourth angel poured out his vial upon the sun; and power was given unto him to scorch men with fire.

And men were scorched with great heat, and blasphemed the name of God, which hath power over these plagues: and they repented not to give him glory.

And the fifth angel poured out his vial upon the seat of the beast; and his kingdom was full of darkness; and they gnawed their tongues for pain,

And blasphemed the God of heaven because of their pains and their sores, and repented not of their deeds.

And the sixth angel poured out his vial upon the great river Euphrates; and the water thereof was dried up, that the way of the kings of the east might be prepared.

And I saw three unclean spirits like frogs come out of the mouth of the dragon, and out of the mouth of the beast, and out of the mouth of the false prophet.

For they are the spirits of devils, working miracles, which go forth unto the kings of the earth and of the whole world, to gather them to the battle of that great day of God Almighty.

Behold, I come as a thief, Blessed is he that watcheth, and keepeth his garments, lest he walk naked, and they see his shame. (Rev. 16:1–15)

In this last line is where Jesus is saying he will return the same as when they came and took him to crucify him. He said, "Are ye come out as against a thief with swords and staves for to take me?"

in Matthew 26:55. He was an innocent man who was falsely accused and taken away as a thief, and so he shall return the same way.

> And he gathered them together into a place called in the Hebrew tongue Armageddon. (Rev. 16:16)

In Hebrew, *Armageddon* means "hill of Megiddo," which is south of present-day Haifa in Israel. Jesus also said in Luke 21:20, "And when ye shall see Jerusalem compassed with armies, then know that the desolation thereof is nigh." *Compassed* means surrounded or enclosed on all sides, which armies now surround Israel. *Desolation* is the state of complete emptiness or destruction that it no longer exists or cannot be repaired.

Let's find out what happens next in this chapter.

> And the seventh angel poured out his vial into the air; and there came a great voice out of the temple of heaven, from the throne, saying, It is done.
>
> And there were voices, and thunders, and lightnings; and there was a great earthquake, such as was not since men were upon the earth, so mighty an earthquake, and so great
>
> And the great city was divided into three parts, and the cities of the nations fell: and great Babylon came in remembrance before God, to give unto her the cup of the wine of the fierceness of his wrath.
>
> And every island fled away, and the mountains were not found.
>
> And there fell upon men a great hail out of heaven, every stone about the weight of a talent: and men blasphemed God because of the plague of the hail; for the plague thereof was exceeding great. (Rev. 16:17–21)

Revelation 17

For God hath put in their hearts to fulfill his will

And there came one of the seven angels which had the seven vials, and talked with me, saying unto me, Come hither; I will shew unto thee the judgment of the great whore that sitteth upon many waters:

With whom the kings of the earth have committed fornication, and the inhabitants of the earth have been made drunk with the wine of her fornication.

So he carried me away in the spirit into the wilderness: and I saw a woman sit upon a scarlet coloured beast, full of names of blasphemy, having seven heads and ten horns.

And the woman was arrayed in purple and scarlet colour, and decked with gold and precious stones and pearls, having a golden cup in her hand full of abominations and filthiness of her fornications:

And upon her forehead was a name written, MYSTERY, BABYLON THE GREAT,

THE MOTHER OF HARLOTS AND ABOMINATIONS OF THE EARTH.

And I saw the woman drunken with the blood of the saints, and with the blood of the martyrs of Jesus: and when I saw her, I wondered with great admiration.

And the angel said unto me Wherefore didst thou marvel? I will tell thee the mystery of the woman and of the beast that carrieth her, which hath the seven heads and ten horns.

The beast that thou sawest was, and is not; and shall ascend out of the bottomless pit, and go into perdition: and they that dwell on the earth shall wonder, whose names were not written in the book of life from the foundation of the world, when they behold the beast that was, and is not, and yet is.

And here is the mind which hath wisdom. The seven heads are seven mountains, on which the woman sitteth.

And there are seven kings: five are fallen, and one is, and the other is not yet come; and when he cometh, he must continue a short space.

And the beast that was, and is not, even he is the eighth, and is of the seven, and goeth into perdition.

And the ten horns which thou sawest are ten kings, which have received no kingdom as yet; but receive power as kings one hour with the beast.

These have one mind, and shall give their power and strength unto the beast.

These shall make war with the Lamb, and the Lamb shall overcome them: for he is Lord of lords, and King of kings: and they that are with him are called, and chosen, and faithful.

> And he saith unto me, The waters which thou sawest, where the whore sitteth, are peoples, and multitudes, and nations, and tongues. (Rev. 17:1–15)

Revelation 17:15 is the only verse that does not have to be interpreted and therefore is a revelation. The angel of the waters mentioned this earlier, where they poured their vials of plagues over the sea, and the rivers and fountains of waters. And now, here, the waters are peoples, multitudes and nations, and tongues. So, something that sounds fantastic in the previous chapter, like turning the sea and rivers and fountains into blood, is now revealed as the plague poured out on a multitude of peoples of multiple nations with multiple languages. Revelation 17:7–14 are all put there to make those who think they are wise fools!

> And the ten horns which thou sawest upon the beast, these shall hate the whore, and shall make her desolate and naked, and shall eat her flesh, and burn her with fire.
>
> For God hath put in their hearts to fulfil his will, and to agree, and give their kingdom unto the beast, until the words of God shall be fulfilled.
>
> And the woman which thou sawest is that great city, which reigneth over the kings of the earth. (Rev. 17:16–18)

Revelation 17:18 is the only other verse that is clear prophecy revealed. The woman is the great city that rules over the rest of the world. You could say the most powerful city is the leader of the world. It is considered the world's only superpower that rules other nations and economies. This city is not one of the United States, yet it is connected to it on the East Coast. The city is laid out in the shape of a pentagram for Satan.

Revelation 18

The end of sorcery

> And after these things I saw another angel
> come down from heaven, having great power;
> and the earth was lightened with his glory.
>   And he cried mightily with a strong voice,
> saying, Babylon the great is fallen, is fallen, and is
> become the habitation of devils, and the hold of
> every foul spirit, and a cage of every unclean and
> hateful bird. (Rev.18:1–2)

Since the ancient city of Babylon has long been destroyed and
the book of Revelation is prophecy, this use of Babylon is rooted
in the Hebrew word *babel*. Babel means a confused noise, typically
that made by a number of voices, which is what God did in Genesis
11:4–9. This is what we have in this city today, the modern-day city
where all the inhabitants "babble" on and on.

> For all nations have drunk of the wine of
> the wrath of her fornications, and the kings of
> the earth have committed fornication with her,
> and the merchants of the earth have committed
> fornication with her, and the merchants of the

earth are waxed rich through the abundance of her delicacies.

And I heard another voice from heaven saying, Come out of her, my people, that ye be not partakers of her sins, and that ye receive not of her plagues.

For her sins have reached unto heaven, and God hath remembered her iniquities.

Reward her even as she rewarded you, and double unto her double according to her works: in the cup which she hath filled fill to her double.

How much she hath glorified herself, and lived deliciously, so much torment and sorrow give her: for she saith in her heart, I sit a queen, and am no widow, and shall see no sorrow.

Therefore shall her plagues come in one day, death, and mourning, and famine; and she shall be utterly burned with fire: for strong is the Lord God who judgeth her.

And the kings of the earth, who have committed fornication and lived deliciously with her, shall bewail her, and lament for her, when they shall see the smoke of her burning.

Standing afar off for the fear of her torment, saying, Alas, alas that great city Babylon, that mighty city! For in one hour is thy judgment come.

And the merchants of the earth shall weep and mourn over her; for no man buyeth their merchandise any more:

The merchandise of gold, and silver, and precious stones, and of pearls, and fine linen, and purple, and silk, and scarlet, and all thyine wood, and all manner vessels of ivory, and all manner vessels of most precious wood, and of brass, and iron, and marble,

And cinnamon, and odours, and ointments, and frankincense, and wine, and oil, and fine flour, and wheat, and beasts, and sheep, and horses, and chariots, and slaves, and souls of men. ["And souls of men" means those who were free and accepted the mark of the beast.]

And the fruits that thy soul lusted after are departed from thee, and all things which were dainty and goodly are departed from thee, and thou shalt find them no more at all.

The merchants of these things, which were made rich by her, shall stand afar off for the fear of her torment, weeping and wailing,

And saying, Alas, alas that great city, that was clothed in fine linen, and purple, and scarlet, and decked with gold, and precious stones, and pearls!

For in one hour so great riches is come to nought. And every shipmaster, and all the company in ships, and sailors, and as many as trade by sea, stood afar off,

And cried when they saw the smoke of her burning, saying, What city is like unto this great city!

And they cast dust on their heads, and cried, weeping and wailing, saying, Alas, alas that great city wherein were made rich all that had ships in the sea by reason of her costliness! For in one hour is she made desolate.

Rejoice over her, thou heaven, and ye holy apostles and prophets; for God hath avenged you on her.

And a mighty angel took up a stone like a great millstone, and cast it into the sea, saying, Thus with violence shall that great city Babylon be thrown down, and shall be found no more at all.

And the voice of harpers, and musicians, and of pipers, and trumpeters, shall be heard

> no more at all in thee; and no craftsman [short
> for "witchcraftsman"], of whatsoever craft he be;
> shall be found any more in thee; and the sound of
> a millstone shall be heard no more at all in thee.
> (Rev. 18:3–22)

In these verses here, the word craft means "The Craft" which by definition is the brotherhood of Freemasons who openly profess that they are the protectors of "the Craft" and were "free and accepted the mark of the beast in their hand [shake] and in their forehead [blood oath always on their mind to not betray Lucifer and their brothers in him]."

You see, one definition of *mark* is "any thing, sign, or symbol that shows ownership of another." This confirms the words afore-mentioned "and souls of men" who "sold" their soul to "live better" and give up living forever. They, the antichrists, or against Christ, are the ones responsible for killing Jesus with their craft, as it says in Mark 14:1: "And the chief priests and the scribes sought how they might take him by *craft* [emphasis mine], and put him to death."

From Genesis to the last page of Revelation, there is sorcery, magic, witches, sorceresses, consulters of familiar spirits, wizards that peep, and so on. They are the reason for the end of this world.

Let's read further what this chapter teaches us.

> And the light of a candle shall shine no
> more at all in thee; and the voice of the bride-
> groom and of the bride shall be heard no more at
> all in thee: for thy merchants were the great men
> of the earth; for by thy sorceries were all nations
> deceived.
>
> And in her was found the blood of proph-
> ets, and of saints, and of all that were slain upon
> the earth. (Rev. 18:23–24)

See? By their sorceries, they made themselves rich, and they and Satan know it will take God's intervention to stop their witchcraft.

Revelation 19

A name written that no man knew but he himself

And after these things I heard a great voice of much people in heaven, saying, Alleluia; Salvation, and glory, and honour, and power, unto the Lord our God:

For true and righteous are his judgments: for he hath judged the great whore, which did corrupt the earth with her fornications, and hath avenged the blood of his servants at her hand.

And again they said, Alleluia. And her smoke rose up for ever and ever.

And the four and twenty elders and the four beasts fell down and worshipped God that sat on the throne, saying, Amen; Alleluia.

And a voice came out of the throne, saying, Praise our God, all ye his servants, and ye that fear him, both small and great.

And I heard as it were the voice of a great multitude, and as the voice of many waters, and as the voice of mighty thunderings, saying, Alleluia: for the Lord God omnipotent reigneth.

Let us be glad and rejoice, and give honour to him: for the marriage of the Lamb is come, and his wife hath made herself ready.

And to her was granted that she should be arrayed in fine linen, clean and white: for the fine linen is the righteousness of the saints.

And he saith unto me, Write, Blessed are they which are called unto the marriage supper of the Lamb. And he saith unto me, These are the true sayings of God.

And I fell at his feet to worship him. And he said unto me, See thou do it not: I am thy fellowservant, and of thy brethren that have the testimony of Jesus: worship God: for the testimony of Jesus is the spirit of prophecy. [Jesus is the spirit of prophecy.]

And I saw heaven opened, and behold a white horse; and he that sat upon him was called Faithful and True, and in righteousness he doth judge and make war.

His eyes were as a flame of fire, and on his head were many crowns; and he hath a name written, that no man knew, but he himself. ["A name written" is the same name written that no one knows but he himself who receives it in Revelation 2:17.]

And he was clothed with a vesture dipped in blood: and his name is called The Word of God.

And the armies which were in heaven followed him upon white horses, clothed in fine linen, white and clean.

And out of his mouth goeth a sharp sword, that with it he should smite the nations: and he shall rule them with a rod of iron: and he treadeth the winepress of the fierceness and wrath of

Almighty God. [This is what Jesus gave to the one who overcomes back in Rev 2:26–28.]

And he hath on his vesture and on his thigh a name written, KING OF KINGS, AND LORD OF LORDS. (Rev. 19:1–16)

This is the revelation of the mystery of the prophecy of the name that no one knows except the one man who receives it. This is mentioned just a few lines ago in Revelation 19:12 and in Revelation 2:17—"And in the stone a new name written, which no man knows except he that receives it."

Remember that if it requires interpretation, it is shortly before or after what requires interpretation. The name written in Revelation 19:12 that no one knows is the same as the name written in the white stone, which I showed you the stone is the Bible and here it is written. Again, Revelation 2:17 says, "And in the stone a new name written, which no man knows except he that receives it," and the name is KING OF KINGS, AND LORD OF LORDS, which is the name written that no one knows except the one who receives it.

And I saw an angel standing in the sun; and he cried with a loud voice, saying to all the fowls that fly in the midst of heaven, Come and gather yourselves together unto the supper of the great God;

That ye may eat the flesh of kings, and the flesh of captains, and the flesh of mighty men, and the flesh of horses, and of them that sit on them, and the flesh of all men, both free and bond, both small and great.

And I saw the beast, and the kings of the earth, and their armies, gathered together to make war against him that sat on the horse, and against his army.

And the beast was taken, and with him the false prophet that wrought miracles before him, with which he deceived them that had received the mark of the beast, and them that worshipped his image. These both were cast alive into a lake of fire burning with brimstone.

And the remnant were slain with the sword of him that sat upon the horse, which sword proceeded out of his mouth [Read Isaiah 11:4: "And he shall smite the earth with the rod of his mouth, and with the breath of his lips shall he slay the wicked."]: and all the fowls were filled with their flesh.

(Rev. 19:17–21)

Fire and brimstone is easy to understand—if you know what a volcano is—and the lava that flows from it creating lakes of fire and exploding with brimstone. Brimstone is the archaic meaning of sulfur, which is in lava. The lake of fire is actually only twenty miles away.

Anywhere on earth that you stand, beneath you is magma, or lava, that burns with fire and sulfur (brimstone). The wicked who are cast there can see through the gulf between us and at the world without a curse, which is what causes them to be "tormented forever," not to mention being able to feel their own soul on fire and not being able to die.

Revelation 20

Every man judged for his works

And I saw an angel come down from heaven, having the key of the bottomless pit and a great chain in his hand.

And he laid hold on the dragon, that old serpent, which is the Devil, and Satan, and bound him a thousand years,

And cast him into the bottomless pit, and shut him up, and set a seal upon him, that he should deceive the nations no more, till the thousand years should be fulfilled: and after that he must be loosed a little season.

And I saw thrones, and they sat upon them, and judgment was given unto them: and I saw the souls of them that were beheaded for the witness of Jesus, and for the word of God, and which had not worshipped the beast, neither his image, neither had received his mark upon their foreheads, or in their hands; and they lived and reigned with Christ a thousand years. (Rev. 20:1–4)

You see, God set a mark upon Cain in Genesis 4:15: "And the LORD said unto him, Therefore whosoever slayeth Cain, vengeance shall be taken on him sevenfold. And the LORD set a mark upon Cain, lest any finding him should kill him." The mark he set upon him was saying to him "Whosoever slayeth Cain, vengeance shall be taken on him sevenfold." He simply said he was a marked man.

But the rest of the dead lived not again until the thousand years were finished. This is the first resurrection.

Blessed and holy is he that hath part in the first resurrection: on such the second death hath no power, but they shall be priests of God and of Christ, and shall reign with him a thousand years. [Remember that one day is as a thousand years and a thousand years are as if one day to God.]

And when the thousand years are expired, Satan shall be loosed out of his prison,

And shall go out to deceive the nations which are in the four quarters of the earth, Gog and Magog, to gather them together to battle: the number of whom is as the sand of the sea.

And they went up on the breadth of the earth, and compassed the camp of the saints about, and the beloved city: and fire came down from God out of heaven, and devoured them.

And the devil that deceived them was cast into the lake of fire and brimstone, where the beast and the false prophet are, and shall be tormented day and night for ever. [This the torment I mentioned earlier, where they look up from the lava lake forever to see the beautiful paradise of God—earth without the curse.]

And I saw a great white throne, and him that sat on it, from whose face the earth and the heaven fled away; and there was found no place for them.

And I saw the dead, small and great, stand before God; and the books were opened: and another book was opened, which is the book of life: and the dead were judged out of those things which were written in the books, according to their works.

And the sea gave up the dead which were in it; and death and hell delivered up the dead which were in them: and they were judged every man according to their works.

And death and hell were cast into the lake of fire. This is the second death.

And whosoever was not found written in the book of life was cast into the lake of fire. (Rev. 20:5–15)

Revelation 21

A new world enlightened by God

And I saw a new heaven and a new earth: for the first heaven and the first earth were passed away; and there was no more sea.

And I John saw the holy city, New Jerusalem, coming down from God out of heaven, prepared as a bride adorned for her husband.

And I heard a great voice out of heaven saying, Behold, the tabernacle of God is with men, and he will dwell with them, and they shall be his people [*his people* means they are no longer the children of God but *his* people], and God himself shall be with them, and be their God.

And God shall wipe away all tears from their eyes; and there shall be no more death, neither sorrow, nor crying, neither shall there be any more pain: for the former things are passed away [the visions in Revelation 21:1—"the first heaven and the first earth were passed away"].

And he that sat upon the throne said, Behold, I make all things new. ["I make all things new" includes the gospel and prophesies of Jesus, read with understanding.] And he said unto me, Write: for these words are true and faithful.

6 And he said unto me, It is done. I am Alpha and Omega, the beginning and the end. I will give unto him that is athirst of the fountain of the water of life freely.

7 He that overcometh [this is the second son who overcame in Revelation 2:7, 11, 17, 26–28 and Revelation 3:5,12, 21] shall inherit all things; and I will be his God, and he shall be my son. (Rev. 21:1–7)

Inherit literally means "receive (money, property, or a title) as an heir at the death of the previous holder." This death was the death of Jesus the man in the flesh, and *all things* means "all things," which is mentioned in Revelation 10:6: "Who created heaven, and the things that therein are, and the earth, and the things that therein are, and the sea, and the things which are therein,"

Jesus gave all things he had, including the morning star ("I am the morning star" [Rev. 22:16], which is the sun, or the title *Son*), to the one who overcame as he did, and God himself is verifying that the one who overcomes inherits everything that he created. This is the race where he was the first to win victory over death in the flesh, and his spirit comes in to another that is the last begotten of the dead.

This is the reason for evil in the world and the people who live in the shadows of the world. This is why the children of the wicked rule this world and rule all churches of every religion so they can keep this hidden mystery a secret to seek it for themselves, thinking they have a chance of stealing God's creation. They will never stand a chance because God must draw, or choose, the one.

Let's continue reading what Revelation 21 offers us.

But the fearful, and unbelieving, and the abominable, and murderers, and whoremonger-ers, and sorcerers, and idolaters, and all liars, shall have their part in the lake which burneth with

fire and brimstone: which is the second death.
(Rev. 21:8)

Notice the first mentioned here is the fearful and unbelieving in the lamb who overcame and has Jesus's new name. It's how many lose their crown of life—by unbelief. Also notice there are still sorcerers on the earth when this comes about. Remember that the kingdom of heaven grows as a mustard seed: it gets built. And especially notice that God separates "all liars" from the rest. This is because he not only hates liars because they are of their father the devil, who was a liar from the beginning and the father of it, but you can't do anything with someone who lies. Also remember that truth and justice prevail in the kingdom.

> And there came unto me one of the seven angels which had the seven vials full of the seven last plagues, and talked with me, saying, Come hither, I will shew thee the bride, the Lamb's wife. [This is the end of the statement about the Lamb's wife, which is kept a mystery for a little longer.]
>
> And he carried me away in the spirit to a great and high mountain, and shewed me that great city, the holy Jerusalem, descending out of heaven from God,
>
> Having the glory of God: and her light was like unto a stone most precious, even like a jasper stone, clear as crystal;
>
> And had a wall great and high, and had twelve gates, and at the gates twelve angels, and names written thereon, which are the names of the twelve tribes of the children of Israel:
>
> On the east three gates; on the north three gates; on the south three gates; and on the west three gates.

And the wall of the city had twelve foundations, and in them the names of the twelve apostles of the Lamb.

And he that talked with me had a golden reed to measure the city, and the gates thereof, and the wall thereof

And the city lieth foursquare, and the length is as large as the breadth: and he measured the city with the reed, twelve thousand furlongs. The length and the breadth and the height of it are equal.

And he measured the wall thereof, an hundred and forty and four cubits, according to the measure of a man, that is, of the angel.

And the building of the wall of it was of jasper: and the city was pure gold, like unto clear glass.

And the foundations of the wall of the city were garnished with all manner of precious stones. The first foundation was jasper; the second, sapphire; the third, a chalcedony; the fourth, an emerald;

The fifth, sardonyx; the sixth, sardius; the seventh, chrysolyte; the eighth, beryl; the ninth, a topaz; the tenth, a chrysoprasus; the eleventh, a jacinth; the twelfth, an amethyst.

And the twelve gates were twelve pearls; every several gate was of one pearl: and the street of the city was pure gold, as it were transparent glass.

And I saw no temple therein: for the Lord God Almighty and the Lamb are the temple of it.

And the city had no need of the sun, neither of the moon, to shine in it: for the glory of God did lighten it, and the Lamb is the light thereof. (Rev. 21:9–23)

The archaic meaning of *lighten* is to "enlighten spiritually." This means that the glory of God did enlighten it. The word *thereof* means "of the thing just mentioned." This means the Lamb is the enlightenment of the glory of God. Do you see the light?

This is all a very descriptive picture of what John saw in the vision. Now imagine for a moment that you are him two thousand years ago, before there was electricity, lights, airplanes and so forth, and you are taken into the future which is today. And let's say you were taken up into the sky in an airplane and flew over a major city and saw it lit up at night. If you never saw anything like this before, and didn't know what made all the city you were flying over glow in the dark, you would probably describe it as he does here in these verses.

> And the nations of them which are saved shall walk in the light [enlightenment] of it: and the kings of the earth do bring their glory and honor into it.
>
> And the gates of it shall not be shut at all by day: for there shall be no night there.
>
> And they shall bring the glory and honor of the nations into it.
>
> And there shall in no wise enter into it any thing that defileth, neither whatsoever worketh abomination, or maketh a lie: but they which are written in the Lamb's book of life. (Rev. 21:24–27)

The lamb's book of life is different from the book of life from the foundation of the world.

Revelation 22

The final chapter

And he shewed me a pure river of water of life, clear as crystal, proceeding out of the throne of God and of the Lamb. [The two are one—God is the spirit manifest in the lamb, hence the Lord of Hosts.]

In the midst of the street of it, and on either side of the river, was there the tree of life, which bare twelve manner of fruits, and yielded her fruit every month: and the leaves of the tree were for the healing of the nations.

And there shall be no more curse: but the throne of God and of the Lamb shall be in it; and his servants shall serve him. [Here, again, we have two—God and the Lamb—which is plural. But we have a singular *him* at the end, hence the two are one, like Jesus said "I and the Father are one."]

And they shall see his face; and his name shall be in their foreheads.

And there shall be no night there; and they need no candle, neither light of the sun; for the Lord God giveth them light: and they (still talking about God and the Lamb) shall reign for ever and ever.

And he said unto me, These sayings are faithful and true: and the Lord God of the holy prophets sent his angel to shew unto his servants the things which must shortly be done.

Behold, I come quickly: blessed is he that keepeth the sayings of the prophecy of this book. ["Blessed is "*he*"—*he* is singular masculine and is referring to the Lamb who was slain, which is the one overcomer who fulfilled all these prophecies.]

And I John saw these things, and heard them. And when I had heard and seen, I fell down to worship before the feet of the angel which shewed me these things.

Then saith he unto me, See thou do it not: for I am thy fellowservant, and of thy brethren the prophets, and of them which keep the sayings of this book: worship God.

And he saith unto me, Seal not the sayings of the prophecy of this book: for the time is at hand. [Now it really is!]

He that is unjust, let him be unjust still: and he which is filthy, let him be filthy still: and he that is righteous, let him be righteous still: and he that is holy, let him be holy still.

And, behold, I come quickly; and my reward is with me, to give every man according as his work shall be.

I am Alpha and Omega, the beginning and the end, the first and the last.

Blessed are they that do his [the Lamb] commandments, that they may have right to the tree of life, and may enter in through the gates into the city.

For without [outside new Jerusalem] are dogs, and sorcerers [sorcerers are still on earth but get kicked out of the city], and whoremongerers, and murderers, and idolaters, and whosoever loveth and maketh a lie.

I Jesus have sent mine angel to testify unto you these things in the churches. I am the root and the offspring of David, and the bright and morning star.

And the Spirit and the bride say, Come. And let him that heareth say, Come. And let him that is athirst come. And whosoever will, let him take the water of life freely. (Rev. 22:1–17)

In the preceding verses, this is where the bride is revealed. The conjunction *and* is used to connect words or the same part of speech, clauses, or sentences that are to be taken jointly. For example, if I say "The *commander in chief* and *president* say 'come,'" I am speaking of the president with two words connected by the conjunction *and*. Now when it says "The Spirit and the Bride say, Come," the Spirit *is* the Bride of the Lamb.

The word *marriage*, by definition, is "any close or intimate union." The root word is *marry*, which means "to join closely or intimately"; "unite." This is the same as Jesus was "married" or closely joined to the Father—"I and the Father are one."

And here in the end of the world, the Spirit of God *is* the Bride of the Lamb who Jesus came into (Rev. 3:20) and granted to sit in his throne, whom he had sat down in his Father's throne (Rev. 3:21); who wrote the name of God, New Jerusalem, and His new name upon (Rev. 3:12); who gave power to rule the nations as he was given of his Father (Rev. 2:26–28); who gave a white stone with a new name written—King of Kings and Lord of Lords (Rev. 2:17; 19:16); and who first gave him immortality by giving to eat of the tree of life in Revelation 2:7.

Let's find out what this final chapter of Revelation says.

For I testify unto every man that heareth the words of the prophecy of this book, If any man shall add unto these things, God shall add unto him the plagues that are written in this book:

And if any man shall take away from the words of the book of this prophecy, God shall take away his part out of the book of life, and out of the holy city, and from the things which are written in this book.

He which testifieth these things saith, Surely I come quickly. Amen. Even so, come, Lord Jesus.

The grace of our Lord Jesus Christ be with you all. Amen. (Rev. 22:18–21)

This is a legally executable document.

About the Author

Forty-five years ago, when he was at the tender age of seven, he heard the scripture from his Sunday school teacher who said, "Seek the Lord while he may be found, and if you shall seek the Lord thy God, you shall find him if you seek him with all thy heart and with all your soul."

This is what he set out to do with his life while raising his two sons and working as a custom carpenter and designing and building custom residential homes.

CPSIA information can be obtained
at www.ICGtesting.com
Printed in the USA
BVHW071152240619
551796BV00004B/615/P

9 781640 030886